THE SOLDIER'S ART

The last jerky, strangled notes of the Warning, as it died away, always recalled some musical instrument inadequately mastered; General Conyers, for example, rendering Gounod or Saint-Saëns on his 'cello, or that favourite of Moreland's (also inclined to play Saint-Saëns), the pirate-like man with an old-fashioned wooden leg and patch over one eye, who used to scrape away at a fiddle in one of the backstreets off Piccadilly Circus. Still sleepy, I began to dress in the dark, since switching on the light in the curtainless bedroom would entail the trouble of rearranging the window's blackout boards. Musical variations of different forms of Air-raid Warning might repay study. Where Isobel was living in the country, the vicar, as chief warden, issued the local Warning in person by telephone. Either to instil the seriousness of the notification, or because intoning came as second nature to one of his calling, he always enunciated the words imitatively, ululating his voice from high to low in paraphrase of a siren:

'. . . Air-raid Warning . . . *Air-raid Warning* . . . Air-raid Warning . . . *Air-raid Warning* . . . Air-raid Warning . . . *Air-raid Warning* . . .'

Such reveries floated out of the shadows of the room, together with the hope that the Luftwaffe, bearing in mind the duration of their return journey, would not protract with too much Teutonic conscientiousness the night's activities.

A Dance to the Music of Time

A Question of Upbringing
A Buyer's Market
The Acceptance World
At Lady Molly's
Casanova's Chinese Restaurant
The Kindly Ones
The Valley of Bones
The Soldier's Art
The Military Philosophers
Books Do Furnish a Room
Temporary Kings
Hearing Secret Harmonies

*All the books in the series
are available from Mandarin Paperbacks*

ANTHONY POWELL

The Soldier's Art

Mandarin

This edition published in the United Kingdom in 1991 by
Mandarin Paperbacks·

3 5 7 9 10 8 6 4 2

Copyright © Anthony Powell 1966

First published in the United Kingdom in 1966 by William Heinemann

Mandarin Paperbacks
Random House UK Limited
20 Vauxhall Bridge Road, London SW1V 2SA

Random House Australia (Pty) Limited
20 Alfred Street, Milsons Point, Sydney
New South Wales 2061, Australia

Random House New Zealand Limited
18 Poland Road, Glenfield, Auckland 10, New Zealand

Random House South Africa (Pty) Limited
Endulini, 5a Jubilee Road, Parktown 2193, South Africa

Random House UK Limited Reg. No. 954009

A CIP catalogue record for this book is available from the British Library

Papers used by Random House UK Limited
are natural, recyclable products made from wood grown in
sustainable forests. The manufacturing processes conform to
the environmental regulations of the country of origin

Printed and bound in the United Kingdom by
Cox & Wyman Ltd, Reading, Berkshire

ISBN 0 7493 0650 5

For Roy Fuller

A DANCE TO THE MUSIC OF TIME

★ ★ ★ ★ ★ ★ ★ ★ ★

THE SOLDIER'S ART

1

WHEN, AT THE START OF the whole business, I bought an army greatcoat, it was at one of those places in the neighbourhood of Shaftesbury Avenue, where, as well as officers' kit and outfits for sport, they hire or sell theatrical costume. The atmosphere within, heavy with menace like an oriental bazaar, hinted at clandestine bargains, furtive even if not unlawful commerce, heightening the tension of an already novel undertaking. The deal was negotiated in an upper room, dark and mysterious, draped with skiing gear and riding-breeches, in the background of which, behind the glass windows of a high display case, two headless trunks stood rigidly at attention. One of these effigies wore Harlequin's diagonally spangled tights; the other, scarlet full-dress uniform of some infantry regiment, allegorical figures, so it seemed, symbolising dualisms of the antithetical stock-in-trade surrounding them . . . Civil and Military . . . Work and Play . . . Detachment and Involvement . . . Tragedy and Comedy . . . War and Peace . . . Life and Death . . .

An assistant, bent, elderly, bearded, with the congruous demeanour of a Levantine trader, bore the greatcoat out of a secret recess in the shadows and reverently invested me within its double-breasted, brass-buttoned, stiffly pleated khaki folds. He fastened the front with rapid bony fingers, doing up the lapels to the throat; then stepped back a couple of paces to judge the effect. In a three-sided full-length looking-glass nearby I, too, critically examined the back view of the coat's shot-at-dawn cut, aware at the same time that soon, like Alice, I was to pass, as it were by virtue of these habiliments, through its panes into a world no less enigmatic.

'How's that, sir?'

'All right, I think.'

'Might be made for you.'

'Not a bad fit.'

Loosening now quite slowly the buttons, one by one, he paused as if considering some matter, and gazed intently.

'I believe I know your face,' he said.

'You do?'

'Was it *The Middle Watch*?'

'Was what the middle watch?'

'The show I saw you in.'

I have absolutely no histrionic talent, none at all, a constitutional handicap in almost all the undertakings of life; but then, after all, plenty of actors possess little enough. There was no reason why he should not suppose the Stage to be my profession as well as any other. Identification with something a shade more profound than a farce of yesteryear treating boisterously of gun-room life in the Royal Navy might have been more gratifying to self-esteem, but too much personal definition at such a point would have been ponderous, out of place. Accepting the classification, however sobering, I did no more than deny having played in that particular knockabout. He helped me out of the sleeves, gravely shaking straight their creases.

'What's this one for?' he asked.

'Which one?'

'The overcoat—if I might make bold to enquire?'

'Just the war.'

'Ah,' he said attentively. '*The War* . . .'

It was clear he had remained unflustered by recent public events, at the age he had reached perhaps disillusioned with the commonplaces of life; too keen a theatre-goer to spare time for any but the columns of dramatic criticism, however indifferently written, permitting no international crises from the news pages to cloud the keenness of aesthetic consideration. That was an understandable outlook.

'I'll bear the show in mind,' he said.

'Do, please.'

'And the address?'

'I'll take it with me.'

Time was short. Now that the curtain had gone up once more on this old favourite—*The War*—in which, so it appeared, I had been cast for a walk-on part, what days were left before joining my unit would be required for dress rehearsal. Cues must not be missed. The more one thought of it, the more apt seemed the metaphor. Besides, clothes, if not the whole man, are a large part of him, especially when it comes to uniform. In a minute or two the parcel, rather a bulky one, was in my hands.

'Tried to make a neat job of it,' he said, 'though I expect the theatre's only round the corner from here.'

'The theatre of war?'

He looked puzzled for a second, then, recognising a mummer's obscure quip, nodded several times in appreciation.

'And I'll wish you a good run,' he said, clasping together his old lean hands, as if in applause.

'Thanks.'

'Good day, sir, and thank *you*.'

I left the shop, allowing a final glance to fall on the pair of flamboyantly liveried dummies presiding from their glass prison over the sombre vistas of coat-hangers suspending tweed and whipcord. On second thoughts, the headless figures were perhaps not antithetical at all, on the contrary, represented 'Honour and Wit, fore-damned they sit', to whom the Devil had referred in the poem. Here, it was true, they stood rather than sat, but precise posture was a minor matter. The point was that their clothes were just right; while headlessness—like depicting Love or Justice blindfold—might well signify the inexorable preordination of twin destinies that even war could not alter. Indeed, war, likely to offer both attributes unlimited range of expression, would also intensify, rather than abate, their ultimate fatality. Musing on this surmise in the pale, grudging sunshine of London in December, a light wan yet intimate, I recognised the off-licence ever memorable for the bottle of port—could the fluid be so designated—that Moreland and I, centuries before, had bought with such high hopes that Sunday afternoon, later so dismally failed to drink.

Looking back from a disturbed, though at the same time monotonous present, those Moreland days seemed positively Arcadian. Even the threatening arbitrament of war (the Prime Minister's rather ornate phrase in his broadcast) had lent a certain macabre excitement to the weeks leading up to the purchase of the greatcoat. Now, some fourteen months later, that day seemed scarcely less remote than the immolation of the port bottle. The last heard of Moreland —from one of Isobel's letters—was that a musical job had taken him to Edinburgh. Even that information had been sent long ago, soon after my own arrival at Division. Since then I had served a million years at these Headquarters, come to possess no life but the army, no master but Widmerpool, no table companions but Biggs and Soper.

Meanwhile, the war itself had passed through various phases, some of them uncomfortable enough: France in defeat: Europe overrun: invasion imminent: the blitz opened over London. In this last aspect—more specifically—Isobel reported, too, a direct hit on Barnby's frescoes in the Donners-Brebner Building, a pictorial memory dim as Barnby himself, now Camouflage Officer on some distant RAF station. Latterly, things had looked up a trifle, in the Western Desert, for example, but in general the situation remained capable of considerable improvement before being regarded as in the least satisfactory. F Mess—defined by Widmerpool as 'low, though not the final dregs of the Divisional Staff'—did not at all alter a sense that much was wrong with the world.

After our first local blitz—when they killed a thousand people, at that stage of the war regarded as quite a large number for a provincial city in a single night—Major-General Liddament, the Divisional Commander, ordered the Defence Platoon (of which I had temporary charge) to mount brens within the billeting area between the sounding of Air-raid Warning and All Clear. This was just a drill, in practice no shooting envisaged, unless exceptional circumstances—dive-bombing, for example—were to arise; Command, of course, operating normal anti-aircraft batteries. Announced by the melancholy dirge of sirens, like ritual wailings at barbarous obsequies, the German planes used to arrive shortly before midnight—it was a long way to come—turning up in principle about half an hour after sleep had descended. They would fly across the town at comparatively high altitude, then, wheeling lower, hum fussily back on their tracks, sometimes dropping an incendiary or two, for luck, in the immediate neighbourhood of the Mess, before passing on to the more serious business of

5

lodging high explosive on docks and shipyards. These circlings over the harbour lasted until it was time to return. On such nights, after weapons were back in the armoury, sections dismissed to the barrack-room, not much residue of sleep was to be recaptured.

The last jerky, strangled notes of the Warning, as it died away, always recalled some musical instrument inadequately mastered; General Conyers, for example, rendering Gounod or Saint-Saëns on his 'cello, or that favourite of Moreland's (also inclined to play Saint-Saëns), the piratelike man with an old-fashioned wooden leg and patch over one eye, who used to scrape away at a fiddle in one of the backstreets off Piccadilly Circus. Still sleepy, I began to dress in the dark, since switching on the light in the curtainless bedroom would entail the trouble of rearranging the window's blackout boards. Musical variations of different forms of Air-raid Warning might repay study. Where Isobel was living in the country, the vicar, as chief warden, issued the local Warning in person by telephone. Either to instil the seriousness of the notification, or because intoning came as second nature to one of his calling, he always enunciated the words imitatively, ululating his voice from high to low in paraphrase of a siren:

'. . . Air-raid Warning . . . *Air-raid Warning* . . . Air-raid Warning . . . *Air-raid Warning* . . . Air-raid Warning . . . *Air-raid Warning* . . .'

Such reveries floated out of the shadows of the room, together with the hope that the Luftwaffe, bearing in mind the duration of their return journey, would not protract with too much Teutonic conscientiousness the night's activities. Tomorrow, a Command three-day exercise opened, when, so far as the Defence Platoon was concerned, sleep might be equally hard to come by. Outside in the street the air was sharp, although by now meagre signs of the spring were appearing in the surrounding countryside, the hedgeless fields partitioned one from another by tumbledown stone walls. The moonlight had to compete with a rapidly increasing range of artificial illumination that made blackout nugatory. Section posts were to be inspected in turn. The guns were already setting up a good deal of noise. Once a minute fragment of shrapnel pattered with a tinny rattle, like attack from a pea-shooter, against the metal of my helmet. The bren section at the corner of the sports field, last to be visited, had their weapon mounted for aircraft action already and revealed, rather apologetically, they had just discharged a burst.

'Got tired of hanging about watching them drop those things,' said Corporal Mantle, 'so we shot down a flare, for goodness' sake.'

His spectacles gave him a learned, scholarly air, out of keeping with such impatience and violent action. He was a young, energetic NCO, whose name was to go in as candidate for a commission, unless the process were thwarted by Colonel Hogbourne-Johnson, recently showing signs of obstruction in that quarter.

'We'll have to account for the rounds.'

'I'll remember that, sir. Had a few in hand, as a matter of fact. Always just as well, in case there's one of those snap inspections of ammo.'

A shapeless, dumpy figure in a mackintosh came towards us out of the night, the garment so long it reached almost to his heels. This turned out to be Bithel. It was impossible to guess why he should be wandering about at this hour of the night in the middle of a raid. As officer in charge of the Mobile Laundry, his duties could scarcely be required at this moment. He came close to us.

7

'You can't sleep with this noise going on,' he said.

He spoke peevishly, as if remedy, easily applicable, had been for some reason disregarded by the authority responsible.

'I've run out of those pills of mine,' he went on. 'Not even sure I'll be able to get them any longer. Gone off the market, like so many other useful commodities these days. Thought it wiser to put on a helmet. Regulation about that anyway, I expect. I didn't know you or any of the rest of Div HQ were on duty on these occasions. Don't Command organise the pom-poms? That's what they're called, I believe. Then there's a Bofors gun. That's ack-ack too, isn't it? Swedish. I ought to know much more about the Royal Artillery and their functions. Don't come your way as an infantryman, though I've picked up a bit since being at Div.'

He smiled uncomfortably, looking, as always, as if he expected a rebuff. Some months before, he had shaved off the untidy moustache worn when—from some forlorn hope of the Territorial Army Reserve—he had first joined our former Battalion. The physical change, more in keeping with his other natural characteristics, additionally emphasised, in a large moonlike face, the unbelievably inexpert adjustment of his false teeth. That Bithel had lasted so comparatively long in charge of the Mobile Laundry was little short of a miracle. Survival was chiefly due to the fact that this unit was attached only for purposes of administrative convenience, never officially part of the Divisional establishment, therefore liable to be removed at short notice. Accordingly, it never received quite the same disciplinary attention; and, in any case, he was lucky in having Sergeant Ablett as subordinate, who probably did most of the administration. Another reason, too, may have played a

8

part in delaying Bithel's dislodgement, ultimately inevitable. He was accustomed to speak enthusiastically of his own affiliations with the theatrical world, boasts reduced on closer examination to having worked as 'front of House', for a few months, at the theatre of the provincial capital where for a time he had existed precariously. The job had come to an end when that playhouse had been transformed into a cinema, but some shreds of Thespian prestige still clung to Bithel, anyway in his own eyes, so that when the officer in charge of the Mobile Bath Unit—traditional impresario of the Divisional Concert Party—went sick in the middle of rehearsal, the enterprise was handed over to Bithel, who, as producer and director, mounted a very tolerable show.

All the same, ejection sooner or later could not be in doubt. Widmerpool, as DAAG conveniently placed for furthering this measure, was anxious to oust Bithel at the first opportunity; undoubtedly would have done so long before had the Laundry been of our own establishment. Widmerpool's disapproval was not only on understandable general grounds, but, in addition, because he had—rather uncharacteristically, since usually well informed on such matters—swallowed Bithel's intermittently propagated myth about being brother of an officer of the same name and regiment who had won a VC in the '14-'18 war. There seemed no reason why even a VC's younger brother should not fall short in commanding a Mobile Laundry, but for some reason, at an earlier stage, Widmerpool's imagination had been temporarily captured by the legend, so that he felt bitterly about it when the story was shown to be patently untrue. Now, Bithel stood gazing at the bren with close attention, as if he had never before seen such a weapon.

'So far as Div HQ are concerned, only the Defence

Platoon stands-to when there's a raid—one of the General's ideas to keep everyone on their toes,' I said.

Bithel nodded gravely at this explanation of why we were on guard over the sports field. As it happened, he and I had hardly spoken since the night when, in his own phrase, he had 'taken a glass too much' after traversing the gas-chamber at the Castlemallock School of Chemical Warfare. The peregrinations of the Laundry, by definition, kept its officer, a subaltern, in a state of almost permanent circuit throughout the formation's area, while my own duties, however trivial, were too numerous and dispersed to offer much time for hobnobbing with other branches of HQ. We had therefore done no more up to that moment than exchange an odd word together, usually as neighbours at periodical assemblies of all Headquarters officers to attend a lecture or listen to harangues delivered from time to time by the General. This was the first occasion we had met without a crowd of other people round about.

'Bit of a sweat to have to get up like this night after night,' he said. 'Shall we take a turn up the field?'

His sympathy was not without a touch of despair. Few officers could have looked less on their toes than himself at that moment.

'Wait till I've checked this bren.'

The section was found correct. Bithel and I strolled across the grass towards a broken-down cricket pavilion or changing room, a small wooden structure, not much more than a hut. The place had been the cause of trouble lately, because Biggs, Staff Officer Physical Training, had mislaid the key just at the moment when the civilian owners of the requisitioned sports field wanted to store benches or garden seats there. Widmerpool had complained greatly of time wasted on this matter, and, with justice, had been very cross with Biggs, to whom the hut and its key had become almost an obsession. I tried the door to see if it had been properly locked again after the key had been found and the seats moved there. It would not open. Biggs must have seen to that.

The noise of the cannonade round about was deepening. An odour like smouldering rubber imposed a rank, unsavoury surface smell on lesser exhalations of soot and smoke. Towards the far side of the town—the direction of the harbour—thin greenish rays of searchlight beam rapidly described wide intersecting arcs backwards and forwards against the eastern horizon, their range ever reducing, ever extending, as they sliced purposefully across each other's tracks. Then, all at once, these several zigzagging angles of light would form an apex on the same patch of sky, creating a small elliptical compartment through which, once in a way, rapidly darted a tiny object, moving like an angry insect confined in a bottle. As if reacting in deliberately regulated unison to the searchlights' methodical fluctuations, shifting masses of cloudbank alternately glowed and faded, constantly redesigning by that means half-a-dozen intricately pastelled compositions of black and lilac, grey and saffron, pink and gold. Out of this resplendent firmament—which, transcendentally speaking, seemed to threaten imminent revelation from on high—slowly descended, like Japanese lanterns at a fête, a score or more of flares released by the raiding planes. Clustered together in twos and threes, they drifted at first aimlessly in the breeze, after a time scarcely losing height, only swaying a little this way and that, metamorphosed into all but stationary lamps, apparently suspended by immensely elongated wires attached to an invisible ceiling. Suddenly, as if at a prearranged signal for the climax of the spectacle—a set-piece at midnight—high swirling clouds of inky smoke rose from below to meet these flickering airborne torches. At ground level, too, irregular knots of flame began to blaze away like a nest of nocturnal forges in the Black Country. All the world was dipped in a livid, unearthly refulgence, theatrical yet sinister, a light neither of night nor day, the penumbra of Pluto's frontiers. The reek of scorched rubber grew more than ever sickly. Bithel fidgeted with the belt of his mackintosh.

'There's been a spot of bother about a cheque,' he said.

'Yours?'

'I think that's what was really keeping me awake as much as lack of those pills. Things may work out all right because I've paid up—borrowed a trifle from the Postal Officer, as a matter of fact—but cheques are always a worry. They ought to be abolished.'

'Perhaps they will after the war.'

'That'll be too late for me,' said Bithel.

He spoke quite seriously.

'Large sum?'

'Matter of a quid or two—but it did bounce.'

'Can't you keep it quiet?'

'I don't think the DAAG knows up to date.'

That was an important factor from Bithel's point of view. Otherwise Widmerpool might find the opportunity for which he was waiting. I was about to commiserate further, when a deep, rending explosion, that seemed to split the earth, sounded above the regular thud-thud-thud of the guns, vibrations of its crash echoing back in throbbing, shuddering waves from the surrounding hills. Bithel shook his head, his attention distracted for the moment from his own troubles, no doubt worrying enough.

'That must have got home,' he said.

'Sounded like it.'

He began to speak again, then for some reason stopped, apparently changing his mind about the way he was going to put a question. Having evidently decided to frame it in a different form, he made the enquiry with conscious diffidence.

'Told me you were a reader—like me—didn't you?'

'Yes, I am. I read quite a lot.'

I no longer attempted to conceal the habit, with all its undesirable implications. At least admitting to it put one in a recognisably odd category of persons from whom less need be expected than the normal run.

'I love a good book when I have the time,' said Bithel. 'St John Clarke's *Match Me Such Marvel*, that sort of thing. Something serious that takes a long time to get through.'

'Never read that one, as it happens.'

Bithel seemed scarcely aware of my answer. St John Clarke's novel was evidently a side issue, not at all the goal at which these ranging shots were aimed. Though rarely possible to guess, when in a mood for intimate conversation, what he would say next, such pronouncements of Bithel's were always worth attention. Something special was on his mind. When he put the next question, there was a kind of fervour in his voice.

'Ever buy magazines like *Chums* and the *Boy's Own Paper* when you were a nipper?'

'Of course—used to read them in bound annuals as a rule. I've a brother-in-law who still does.'

It was Erry's only vice, though one he tried to keep dark, as showing in himself a lack of earnestness and sense of social obligation. Bithel made some reply, but a sudden concentrated burst of ack-ack fire, as if discharged deliberately for that purpose, drowned his utterance.

'What was that you said?'

Bithel spoke again.

'Still can't hear.'

He came closer.

'. . . hero . . .' he shouted.

'You feel a hero?'

'No . . . I . . .'

The noise lessened, but he still had to yell at the top of his voice to make himself heard.

'. . . always imagined myself the hero *of those serials*.'

The shouted words were just audible above the clatter of guns. He seemed to think they offered a piece of unparalleled psychological revelation on his own part.

'Every boy does,' I yelled back.

'Everyone?'

He was disappointed at that answer.

'I'm sure my brother-in-law does to this day.'

Bithel was not at all interested in my own, or anyone else's, brother-in-law's tendency to self-identification while reading fiction. That was reasonable, because he knew nothing of Erridge's existence. Besides, he wanted only to talk about himself. Although wholly concentrated on that subject, he remained at the same time apologetic as well as intense.

'Only I was thinking the other night—when Jerry first came over—that I was having the very experience I used to read about as a lad.'

'How do you mean?'

' "Coming under fire for the first time"—that was always a great moment in the hero's career. You must remember. Where he "showed his mettle", as the story usually put it.'

He laughed, as if trying to excuse such reckless flights

of fancy, in doing so displaying the double row of Low Comedy teeth.

' "The rattle of musketry from distant hills"—"a little shower of sand churned up by a bullet in front of the redoubt"?'

These conventional phrases from boys' adventure stories might encourage Bithel to plunge further into observations about life. The clichés did indeed stir him.

'That's it,' he said, speaking with much more animation than usual, 'that's just what I meant. Wonderful memory you've got. What you said brings those yarns right back. I was a great reader as a lad. One of those thoughtful little boys. Never kept it up as I should.'

This was a shade reminiscent of Gwatkin, my former Company Commander, poring secretly in the Company office over the *Hymn to Mithras*; but, whereas Gwatkin had meditated such literary material as a consequence of his own infatuation with the mystique of a soldier's life, Bithel's ruminations were quite other. In Bithel, memory of his former partiality for tales of military prowess merely gave rise to a very natural surprise that he was not himself more personally frightened at this moment of comparative danger.

'Strictly speaking, one experienced raids—coming under fire, if you like—when still reading the *Boy's Own Paper*. During the earlier war, I mean.'

'Oh, I didn't,' said Bithel. 'The Zeppelins never came near any of the places we lived when I was a kid. That's just why I was surprised not to mind this sort of thing more. I'm the nervy type, you see. I once had to give evidence in court, rather a nasty case—nothing to do with me, I'm glad to say, just a witness—and I thought my legs were going to give way under me. But this business we're listening to now really doesn't worry me. Worst moment's when the Warning goes, don't you think?'

The question of fear inevitably propounds itself from time to time if a state of war exists. Will circumstances arise when its operation on the senses might become uncomfortably hard to control? Like Bithel, I, too, had thought a certain amount about that subject, reaching the very provisional conclusion that fear itself was less immediately related to unavoidable danger than might at first be supposed; although no doubt that danger, more or less indefinitely increased in motive power, might—indeed certainly would—cause the graph to rise steeply. In bed at night, months before the blitz struck the locality, I would occasionally feel something like abject fear, turning this way and that in my sleeping-bag, for no special reason except that life seemed so utterly out of joint. That was a kind of nervous condition—as Bithel had said of himself—perfectly imaginable in time of peace; perhaps even experienced then, now forgotten, like so much else of that lost world. In the same way, I would sometimes lie awake enduring torments of thwarted desire, depraved fantasies hovering about the camp-bed, reveries of concupiscence that seemed specifically generated by unprepossessing military surroundings. Indeed, it was often necessary to remind oneself that low spirits, disturbed moods, sense of persecution, were not necessarily the consequence of serving in the army, or being part of a nation at war, with which all-inclusive framework depressive mental states now seemed automatically linked.

The raid in progress at that moment was, as Bithel had indicated, more spectacular than alarming, even a trifle stimulating now one was fully awake and dressed; so long as the mind did not dwell on the tedium of a three-day exercise the following day, undertaken after a missed night's sleep. On the other hand, if bombs began to fall in the sports field, such light-hearted impressions might easily deteriorate, especially if the bren were knocked out, removing chance of retaliation. (It might be added that all sense of excitement was to evaporate from air-raids three or four years later.) However, Bithel had ceased to require comment on his own meditations about 'baptism of fire'. He now returned to those personal worries, predominantly financial, which were never far from his mind.

'I do hope things will be OK about that cheque,' he said. 'It all started with the Pay Department being late that month in paying Field Allowance into my banking account.'

This situation did, indeed, arise from time to time, owing to absence of method, possibly downright incompetence, on the part of the Financial Branch of the War Office concerned; possibly due to economic ineptitudes, or ingrained malice, of what Pennistone used later to call the 'cluster of highly educated apes' ultimately in charge of such matters at the Treasury. Whatever the cause, the army from time to time had to forego its wages; sometimes such individual disasters as Bithel's resulting.

'I can see there'll be a fuss,' he said, 'but with any luck it won't come to a court-martial.'

Two or three lesser reports, each thunderous enough, had followed the last big explosion. Now noise was diminishing, the barrage gradually, though appreciably, reducing its volume. Quite suddenly the guns fell entirely silent, like dogs in the night, which, after keeping you awake for hours by their barking, suddenly decide to fall asleep instead. There was a second or two of absolute stillness. Then in the far distance the bell of a fire-engine or ambulance clanged desperately for a time, until the echoes died sadly away on the wind. This discordant ringing was followed by a great clamour, shouts, starting-up of trucks, hooting . . . *the sound of horns and motors, which shall bring Sweeney to Mrs Porter in the spring.* . . . Huge smuts, like giant moths exploring the night air, pervaded its twilight. The smell of burning rubber veered towards a scent more specifically chemical in character, in which the fumes of acetylene seemed recognisable. The consolatory, long drawn out drone came at last. At its first note, as if thus signalled, large drops of rain began to fall. In a minute or two the shower was coming down in buckets, the freshness of the newly wet grass soon obtruding on the other scents.

'Buck up and get that bren covered, Corporal.'

'Shall we pack it in now, sir?'

'Go ahead.'

'Think I'll return to bed too,' said Bithel. 'Doubt if I'll get much sleep. Glad I brought a mac with me now. Need it more than a helmet really. Awful climate over here. Makes you swill down too much of that porter, as they call it. More than you can afford. Just to keep the damp out of your bones. Come and see us in G Mess some time. You'd like Barker-Shaw, the Field Security Officer. He's a professor—philosophy, I think—at one of the 'varsities. Can't remember which. Clever face. The bloke in charge of the Hygiene Section is a bright lad too. You should hear him chaffing the Dental Officer about sterility.'

Our several ways parted. Corporal Mantle marched off his men to the barrack-room. I completed the rounds of the other bren sections, dismissed them, made for bed.

F Mess was only a few minutes' walk from the last of these posts. The Mess was situated in a redbrick, semi-detached villa, one of the houses of a side-street sloping away towards the perimeter of the town. Entering the front door, you were at once assailed by a nightmare of cheerlessness and squalor, all the sordid melancholy, at its worst, of any nest of bedrooms where only men sleep; a prescript of nature unviolated by the character of solely male-infested sleeping quarters established even in buildings hallowed by age and historical association. F Mess was far from such; at least any history to be claimed was in the making. From its windows in daytime, beyond the suburbs, grey, stony hills could be seen, almost mountains; in another direction, that of the docks over which the blitz had been recently concentrating, rose cranes and factory chimneys beyond which inland waters broadened out towards the sea—'the unplumb'd, salt, estranging sea.' About half a mile away from the Mess, though still in the same predominantly residential area, two or three tallish houses accommodated all but the ancillary services of Divisional Headquarters. A few scattered university buildings in the same neighbourhood failed to impart any hint of academic flavour.

'No room in this bloody Mess as it is,' said Biggs, Staff Officer Physical Training, expressing this opinion when I first turned up there. 'Now you come along and add to the crowd, Jenkins, making an extra place at that wretched rickety table we've been issued with to eat off, and another body to occupy the tin sink on the top floor they call a bath—no shaving in the bathroom, remember, absolutely *verboten*. What are you supposed to be doing at Div anyway?'

A captain with '14–'18 ribbons, bald as an egg, he had perhaps been good-looking in a heavy classical manner when younger; anyway, had himself so supposed. Now, with chronically flushed cheeks, he was putting on flesh, his large bulbous nose set between fierce frightened eyes and a small cupid's bow mouth that kept twitching open and shut like a rubber valve. Muscular over-development of chest, shoulder and buttock gave him the air of a strong man at a circus—a strong woman almost—or professional weight-lifter about to present an open-air act to a theatre queue. His voice, harsh and unsure, registered the persecution mania that beset him, that condition, not uncommon in the army, of for ever expecting a superior to appear—bursting like the Demon King out of a trapdoor in the floor—and find fault. In civilian life sports organiser at a seaside resort, Biggs, so I learnt later, was in process of divorcing his wife, a prolonged undertaking, troublesome and expensive, of which he would often complain.

'I'm attached to the DAAG's office.'

'How long for?'

'Don't know.'

'How's Major Widmerpool got authority for an assistant, I should like to know?'

'War Office Letter.'

'Go on.'

'It's to help clear up a lot of outstanding stuff like court-martial proceedings and requisition claims.'

'I've got a lot of outstanding stuff too,' said Biggs. 'A bloody lot. I'm not given an assistant. Well, I don't envy you, Jenkins. It's a dog's life. And don't forget this. Don't forget it. There's nothing lower in the whole bloody army than a second-lieutenant. Other Ranks have got their rights, a one-pipper's none. That goes especially for a Div HQ, and what's more Major Widmerpool is a stickler for having things done the right way. He's been on my own track before now, I can tell you, about procedure he didn't consider correct. He's a devil for procedure.'

After that Biggs lost interest in what was not, indeed, a very interesting subject, except in the light indicated, that to acquire an understrapper at all was, on Widmerpool's part, an achievement worthy of respect. No one but a tireless creator of work for its own sake would have found an assistant necessary in his job, nor, it could be added, in the ordinary course of things been allowed one, even if required. Widmerpool had brought that off. As it happened, a junior officer surplus to establishment was to some extent justified additionally, not long before my arrival at Division, by Prothero, commanding the Defence Platoon, falling from his motor-bicycle and breaking his leg. While he was in hospital I was allotted some of Prothero's duties as well as those delegated by Widmerpool.

'You'll find there's a lot of work to do here,' said Widmerpool, on my first morning. 'A great deal. We shall be at it to a late hour most nights.'

This warning turned out to be justified. There were, as it happened, several courts-martial pending, and another, convened in the past, the findings of which Widmerpool considered unsatisfactory in law. A soldier, who had temporarily gone off his head and assaulted two civilians, had been acquitted at his trial. Widmerpool was engaged in a complicated correspondence on this matter with the Judge Advocate General's Department. Such things took up time, as most of the week was spent out of doors on exercises. Although, since days when we had been at school together, I had been seeing him on and off—very much on and off—for more than twenty years by this time, I found when I worked under him there were still comparatively unfamiliar sides to Widmerpool. Like most persons viewed through the eyes of a subordinate, his nature was to be appreciated with keener insight from below. This new angle of observation revealed, for example, how difficult he was to work with, particularly on account of a secretiveness that derived from perpetual fear, almost obsession, that tasks completed by himself might be attributed to the work of someone else. On that first morning at Division, Widmerpool spoke at length of his own methods. He was already sitting at his table when I arrived in the room. Removing his spectacles, he began to polish them vigorously, assuming at the same time a manner of hearty military geniality.

'No excuses required,' he said, before I could speak. 'Your master is always the first staff officer to arrive at these Headquarters in the morning, and, apart from those on night duty, the last to leave after the sun has gone down. Now I want to explain certain matters before I go off to attend A & Q's morning conference. The first thing is that I never turn work away, neither in the army nor anywhere else. To turn work away is always an error. Never let me find you doing that—unless, of course, it is work another branch is wrongly trying to foist on us, for which they themselves will ultimately reap the credit. A man fond of stealing credit for other people's work is Farebrother, my opposite number at Command. I do not care for Farebrother. He is too smooth. Besides, he is always trying to get even with me about a certain board-meeting in the City we both once attended.'

'I met Farebrother years ago.'

'So you keep on telling me. You mentioned the fact at least once last night. Twice, I think.'

'Sorry.'

'I hope previous acquaintance will prevent you being taken in by his so-called charm, should you have dealings with him as my representative.'

Widmerpool's feud with Sunny Farebrother, so I found, was of old standing, dating back to long before this, though, militarily speaking, in especial to the period when

Farebrother had been brigade-major to Widmerpool's Territorials soon after the outbreak of war. The work of the 'A' staff, which Widmerpool (under 'A & Q', Colonel Pedlar) represented at Division, comprised administration of 'personnel' and 'interior economy', spheres in which, so it appeared, Farebrother had more than once thwarted Widmerpool, especially in such matters as transfers from one unit to another, candidates for courses and the routine of disciplinary cases. Farebrother was, for example, creating difficulties about Widmerpool's correspondence with the Judge Advocate's Department. There were all kind of ways in which an 'opposite number' at Corps or Command could make things awkward for a staff officer at Division. As Command Headquarters were established in one of the blocks of regular army barracks on the other side of the town, I had no contact with Farebrother in the flesh, only an occasional word on the telephone when the DAAG was not available; so the matter of our having met before had never arisen. It was hard to estimate how justly, or otherwise, Widmerpool regarded this mutual relationship. Farebrother's voice on the line never showed the least trace of irritation, even when in warm conflict as to how some order should be interpreted. That quiet demeanour was an outstanding feature of Sunny Farebrother's tactic. On the whole, honours appeared fairly evenly divided between the two of them where practical results were concerned.

'Right, Sunny, right,' Widmerpool would mutter, gritting his teeth when he had sustained a defeat.

'It's gone the way Kenneth wants,' was Farebrother's formula for accepting the reverse situation.

Then there were my own hopes and fears. Though by now reduced to the simplest terms, these were not without complication. In the first place, I desired to separate myself

23

from Widmerpool; at the same time, if possible, achieve material improvement in my own military condition. However, as the months went by, no prospect appeared of liberation from Widmerpool's bottle-washing, still less of promotion. After all, I used to reflect, the army was what you wanted, the army is what you've got—in terms of Molière, *le sous-lieutenant Georges Dandin*. No use to grumble, not to mention the fact that a great many people, far worse off, would have been glad of the job. This was a change, of course, from taking pride in the thought that only luck and good management had brought a commission at all at a moment when so many of my contemporaries were still failing to achieve that. However, to think one thing at one moment, another at the next, is the prescriptive right of every human being. Besides, I recognised the fact that those who desire to share the faint but perceptible inner satisfaction of being included, however obscurely, within the armed forces in time of war, must, if in their middle thirties and without any particular qualifications for practising its arts, pay for that luxury, so far as employment is concerned, by taking what comes. Consolation was to be found, if at all, in Vigny's views (quoted that time in the train by David Pennistone) on the theme of the soldier's 'abnegation of thought and action'.

All the same, although the soldier might abnegate thought and action, it has never been suggested that he should abnegate grumbling. There seemed no reason why I alone, throughout the armies of the world, should not be allowed to feel that military life owed me more stimulating duties, higher rank, increased pay, simply because the path to such ends was by no means clear. Even if Widmerpool left Divisional Headquarters for what he himself used to call 'better things', my own state, so far from improving, would almost certainly be worsened. The Battalion, made up to strength with a flow of young officers increasingly available, would no longer require my services as platoon commander, still less be likely to offer a company. Indeed, those services, taking them all in all, were not to be exaggerated in value to a unit set on streamlining its efficiency. I was prepared to admit that myself. On the other hand, without ordination by way of the War Intelligence Course, or some similar apostleship, there was little or no likelihood of capturing an appointment here or on any other staff. For a course of that sort I should decidedly not be recommended so long as Widmerpool found me useful. When, for one reason or another, that subjective qualification ceased to be valid—when, for example, Widmerpool went to 'better things'—it looked like pretty certain relegation to the Regiment's Infantry Training Centre, a fate little to be desired, and one unlikely to lead to name and fame. Widmerpool himself was naturally aware of these facts. Once, in an expansive mood, he had promised to arrange a future preferable to assignment—as an object to be won, rather than as a competitor—to the lucky-dip provided by an ITC.

'I look after people who've been under me,' Widmerpool said, in the course of cataloguing some of his own good qualities. 'I'll see you get fixed up in a suitable job when I move up the ladder myself. That shouldn't be long now, I opine. At very least I'll get you sent on a course that will make you eligible for the right sort of employment. Don't worry, my boy, I'll keep you in the picture.'

That was a reasonable assurance in the circumstances, and, I felt, not undeserved. 'Putting you in the picture', that relentlessly iterated army phrase, was a special favourite of Widmerpool's. He had used it when, on my first arrival at Headquarters, he had sketched in for me the characteristics of the rest of the Divisional staff. Widmerpool had begun with General Liddament himself.

'Those dogs on a lead and that hunting horn stuck in the blouse of his battle-dress are pure affectation,' he said. 'Come near to being positively undignified in my opinion. Still, of the fifteen thousand men in the Division, I can think of only one other fit to command it.'

'Who is?'

'Modesty forbids my naming him.'

Widmerpool allowed some measure of jocularity to invest his tone when he said that, which increased, rather than diminished, the impression that he spoke with complete conviction. The fact was he rather feared the General. That was partly on account of General Liddament's drolleries, some of which were indeed hard to defend; partly because, when in the mood, the Divisional Commander liked to tease his officers. Widmerpool did not like being teased. The General was not, I think, unaware of Widmerpool's qualities as an efficient, infinitely industrious DAAG, while at the same time laughing at him as a man. In this Widmerpool was by no means his only victim. Generals are traditionally represented as stupid men, sometimes with good reason; though Pennistone, when he talked of such things later, used to argue that the pragmatic approach of the soldier in authority—the basis of much of this imputation—is required by the nature of military duties. It is an approach which inevitably accentuates any individual lack of mental flexibility, an ability, in itself, to be found scarcely more among those who have risen to eminence in other vocations; anyway when operating outside their own terms of reference. In General Liddament, so I was to discover, this pragmatic approach, even if paramount, was at the same time modified by notable powers of observation. A bachelor, devoted to his profession, he was thought to have a promising future ahead of him. Earlier in the war he had been wounded in action with a battalion, a temporary disability that probably accounted for his not already holding a command in the field.

When the General himself was present, Widmerpool was prepared to dissemble his feelings about the two attendant dogs (he disliked all animals), which could certainly become a nuisance when their double-leashed lead became entangled between the legs of staff officers and their clerks in the passages of Headquarters. All the same, Widmerpool was not above saying 'wuff-wuff' to the pair of them, if their owner was in earshot, which he would follow up by giving individual, though unconvincing, pats of encouragement.

'Thank God, the brutes aren't allowed out on exercise,' he said. 'At least the General draws the line there. I think Hogbourne-Johnson hates them as much as I do. Now Hogbourne-Johnson is a man you must take care about. He is bad-tempered, unreliable, not more than averagely efficient and disliked by all ranks, including the General. However, *I* can handle him.'

Hogbourne-Johnson, a full colonel with red tabs, was in charge of operational duties, the staff officer who represented the General in all routine affairs. A Regular, decorated with an MC from the previous war, he was tall, getting decidedly fat, with a small beaky nose set above a pouting mouth turning down at the corners. He somewhat resembled an owl, an angry, ageing bird, recently baulked of a field-mouse and looking about for another small animal to devour. The MC suggested that he was presumably a brave man, or, at very least, one who had experienced enough active service to make that term almost beside the point. Widmerpool acknowledged these earlier qualities.

'Hogbourne-Johnson's had a disappointing career up to date,' he said. 'Unrealized early hopes. At least that's his own opinion. Sword of Honour at Sandhurst, all that sort of thing. Then he made a balls-up somewhere—in Palestine, I think—just before the war. However, he hasn't by any means given up. Still thinks he'll get a Division. If he asked me, I could tell him he's bound for some administrative backwater, and lucky if he isn't bowler-hatted before the cessation of hostilities. The General's going to get rid of him as soon as he can lay hands on the particular man he wants.'

'But the General could sack him tomorrow.'

'For some reason it doesn't suit him to do that. Hogbourne-Johnson is also given to putting on a lot of swank about being a Light Infantryman. To tell the truth, I'm surprised any decent Line regiment could put up with him. They might at least have taught him not to announce himself to another officer on the telephone as "*Colonel* Hogbourne-Johnson". I know Cocksidge says, "This is *Captain* Cocksidge speaking", if he's talking to a subaltern. You expect that from Cocksidge. Hogbourne-Johnson is supposed to know better. The CRA doesn't say, "This is *Brigadier* Hawkins", he says "Hawkins here". However, I suppose I shouldn't grumble. I can manage the man. That's the chief thing. If he hasn't learn how to behave by now, he never will.'

All this turned out to be a pretty just description of Colonel Hogbourne-Johnson and his demeanour, from which in due course I saw no reason to dissent. The army is a place where simple characterisation flourishes. An officer or man is able, keen, well turned out; or awkward, idle, dirty. He is popular or detested. In principle, at any rate, few intermediate shades of colour are allowed to the military spectrum. To some extent individuals, by the very force of such traditional methods of classification, fall into these hard and fast categories. Colonel Hogbourne-Johnson was one of the accepted army types, disappointed, sour, on the look-out for trouble; except by his chief clerk, Diplock, not much loved. On the other hand, although he may have had his foolish moments as well as his disagreeable ones, Hogbourne-Johnson was not a fool. Where Widmerpool, as it turned out, made a mistake, was in supposing he had Colonel Hogbourne-Johnson eating out of his hand. The Colonel's failings, such as they were, did not include total lack of grasp of what Widmerpool himself was like in his dealings. Indeed, Hogbourne-Johnson showed comparatively deep understanding of Widmerpool eventually, when the titanic row took place about Diplock, merging—so far as Widmerpool and Hogbourne-Johnson were concerned—into the question of who was to command the Divisional Reconnaissance Regiment.

The Reconnaissance Unit, then in process of generation, was one in which Colonel Hogbourne-Johnson took a special interest from the start, though not an entirely friendly interest.

'These Recce fellows are doing no more than we Light Bobs used to bring off on our flat feet,' he would remark. 'Nowadays they want a fleet of armoured vehicles for their blasted operations and no expense spared. There's a lot of damned nonsense talked about this so-called Recce Battalion.'

The Reconnaissance Corps—as in due course it emerged

—was indeed, on first coming into being, a bone of considerable contention among the higher authorities. Some pundits thought like Colonel Hogbourne-Johnson; others, just the opposite. One aspect of the question turned on whether the Recce Corps—to some extent deriving in origin from the Anti-tank Companies of an earlier phase of the war—should be used as a convenient limbo for officers, competent, but judged, for one reason or another, less than acceptable in their parent unit; or, on the other hand, whether the Corps should be moulded into one of the élites of the army, having its pick of the best officers and men available. Yanto Breeze, for example, of my former Battalion, had transferred to an Anti-tank Company after the never-explained death—suicide or murder—of Sergeant Pendry. Breeze had been implicated only to the extent of being Orderly Officer that night, sufficient contact—bringing the unpleasantness of a Court of Inquiry—to make him want to leave the Battalion. A good, though not particularly ornamental officer, he was felt to be entirely suitable for the Anti-tank Company. Adherents of a more stylish Recce Corps might, rightly or wrongly, have required rather more outward distinction from their officer in-take than Breeze could show. That was much how things stood. The whole question also appealed greatly to Widmerpool, both as an amateur soldier in relation to tactical possibilities, and, as a professional trafficker in intrigue, a vehicle offering all sorts of opportunity for personal interference.

'Hogbourne-Johnson is playing a double game about the Recce Corps,' he said. 'I happen to know that. The Divisional Commander is very keen on this new unit. The Generals at Corps and Command, on the other hand, are neither of them enthusiastic on the subject, not helpful about speeding things up. Hogbourne-Johnson thinks—in my opinion rightly—that General Liddament plans to get rid of him. Accordingly, he is doing his best to suck up to the other two Generals by backing their policy. He'll then expect help if relieved of his appointment.'

'Like the Unjust Steward.'

'Who was he?'

'In the Bible.'

'I thought you meant an officer of that name.'

'The one who said write ten, when it ought to have been fifty.'

'There's nothing unjust about it,' said Widmerpool, always literal-minded. 'Naturally Hogbourne-Johnson has to obey his own Divisional Commander's orders. I do not for a moment suggest he is overstepping the bounds of discipline. After all, Recce developments are a matter of opinion. A regular officer of his standing has a perfect right to hold views. However, what our General would not be specially pleased to hear is that Hogbourne-Johnson is also moving heaven and earth to get a friend from his own regiment appointed to this new unit's command.'

'How do you know?'

'Because I too have my candidate.'

'To command the Recce Corps?'

'Going into the matter, I discovered Hogbourne-Johnson's tracks. However, I can circumvent him.'

Widmerpool smiled and nodded in a manner to indicate extreme slyness.

'Who?'

'No one you would have met. An excellent officer of my acquaintance called Victor Upjohn. Knew him as a Territorial. First-rate man.'

'Won't they appoint a cavalryman, in spite of Hogbourne-Johnson and yourself?'

'They'll appoint my infantryman—and be glad of him.'

'If the General is likely to be annoyed about Hogbourne-Johnson messing about behind his back as to appointments to command in his Division, he'll be even less pleased to find you at the same game.'

'He won't find out. Neither will Hogbourne-Johnson. Upjohn will simply be gazetted. In the meantime, so far as it goes, I am prepared to play ball with Hogbourne-Johnson up to a point. After all, if I know the right man to command the Recce Corps, it's surely my duty to get him there.'

There was something to be said for this view. If you want your own way in the army, or elsewhere, it is no good following the rules too meticulously, a canon all great military careers—and most civil ones—abundantly illustrate. What Widmerpool had not allowed for, as things turned out, was a sudden deterioration of his own relations with Colonel Hogbourne-Johnson. No doubt one reason for his assurance about that, in spite of the Colonel's uncertain temper, was that most of Widmerpool's dealings were with his own immediate superior, Colonel Pedlar, so less likelihood of friction existed in the other more explosive quarter. Naturally he was in touch with Colonel Hogbourne-Johnson from time to time, but there was no day-to-day routine, during which Hogbourne-Johnson was likely, sooner or later, to make himself disagreeable as a matter of principle.

Colonel Pedlar, as 'A & Q', set no problem at all. Also a regular full colonel with an MC, he had little desire to be unaccommodating for its own sake. A certain stiffness of manner in official transactions was possibly due to appre-

hension that more might be required of him than he had
to offer, rather than an innate instinct, like Hogbourne-
Johnson's, to be unreasonable in all his dealings. Colonel
Pedlar seemed almost surprised to have reached the rank
he had attained; appeared to possess little or no ambition to
rise above it, or at least small hope that he would in due
course be promoted to a brigade. The slowness of his
processes of thought sometimes irked his subordinate,
Widmerpool, even though these processes were on the
whole reliable. If Colonel Hogbourne-Johnson looked like
an owl, Colonel Pedlar resembled a retriever, a faithful
hound, sound in wind and limb, prepared to tackle a dog
twice his size, or swim through a river in spate to collect
his master's game, but at the same time not in the top
class for picking up a difficult scent.

Trouble with Colonel Hogbourne-Johnson might never
have arisen, as it did at that particular moment, had not
Colonel Pedlar been, quite by chance, out of the way.
When it came, sudden and violent, the cause was a far
more humdrum matter than the clandestine guiding of
appointments. Indeed, the incident itself was such a minor
one, so much part of the day's work, that, had I not myself
witnessed it—owing to the exceptional occurrence of
Advance Headquarters and Rear Headquarters being
brought together in one element at the close of the three-
day exercise—I should always have believed some essential
detail to have been omitted from the subsequent story;
guessed that nothing so trivial in itself could have so much
discomposed Widmerpool. That incredulity was due, I
suppose, to underestimation, even after the years I had
known him, of Widmerpool's inordinate, almost morbid,
self-esteem.

During 'schemes', the Defence Platoon was responsible

for guarding the Divisional Commander's Advance Headquarters. This meant, on these occasions, accommodation for myself in the General's Mess; accordingly, temporary disengagement from Widmerpool, whose duties as DAAG focussed on Rear Headquarters. On the last evening of this particular exercise, the Command three-day one, Advance HQ had been established, as usual, in a small farmhouse, one of the scattered homesteads lying in the forbidding countryside of the Command's north-western area, right up in the corner of the map. The first fifty-six hours had been pretty active—as foreseen by me the night before we set out—giving little chance of sleep. However, by the time the General and his operational staff sat down to a late meal at the end of the third day, there was a feeling abroad that the main exertions of the exercise might reasonably be regarded as at an end. Everyone could take things easy for a short time. The General himself was in an excellent temper, the battle against the Blue Force to all intents won.

A single oil lamp threw a circle of dim light round the dining table of the farm parlour where we ate, leaving the rest of the room in heavy shadow, dramatising by its glow the central figures of the company present. Were they a group of conspirators—something like the Gunpowder Plot —depicted in the cross-hatchings of an old engraved illustration? It was not exactly that. At the same time the hard lights and shades gave the circle of heads an odd, mysterious unity. The faces of the two colonels, bird and beast, added a note deliberately grotesque, surrealist, possibly indicating a satirical meaning on the part of the artist, a political cartoonist perhaps. The colonels were placed on either side of General Liddament, who sat at the head of the table, deep in thought. His thin, cleanshaven, ascetic

34

features, those of a schoolmaster or priest—also a touch of Sir Magnus Donners—were yellowish in complexion. Perhaps that tawny colour clarified the imagery, for now it became plain.

Here was Pharaoh, carved in the niche of a shrine between two tutelary deities, who shielded him from human approach. All was manifest. Colonel Hogbourne-Johnson and Colonel Pedlar were animal-headed gods of Ancient Egypt. Colonel Hogbourne-Johnson was, of course, Horus, one of those sculptured representations in which the Lord of the Morning Sun resembles an owl rather than a falcon; a bad-tempered owl at that. Colonel Pedlar's dog's muzzle, on the other hand, was a milder than normal version of the jackal-faced Anubis, whose dominion over Tombs and the Dead did indeed fall within A & Q's province. Some of the others round about were less easy to place in the Egyptian pantheon. In fact, one came finally to the conclusion, none of them were gods at all, mere bondsmen of the temple. For example, Cocksidge, officer responsible for Intelligence duties, with his pale eager elderly-little-boy expression— although on the edge of thirty—was certainly the lowest of slaves, dusting only exterior, less sacred precincts of the shrine, cleaning out with his hands the priest's latrine, if such existed on the temple premises. Next to Cocksidge sat Greening, the General's ADC, pink cheeked, fair haired, good-natured, about twenty years old, probably an alien captive awaiting sacrifice on the altar of this anthropomorphic trinity. Before anyone else could be satisfactorily identified, Colonel Pedlar spoke.

'How went the battle, Derrick?' he asked.

There had been silence until then. Everyone was tired. Besides, although Colonel Hogbourne-Johnson and Colonel Pedlar were not on notably good terms with each other, they felt rank to inhibit casual conversation with subordinates. Both habitually showed anxiety to avoid a junior officer's eye at meals in case speech might seem required. To make sure nothing so inadvertent should happen, each would uninterruptedly gaze into the other's face across the table, with all the fixedness of a newly engaged couple, eternally enchanted by the charming appearance of the other. The colonels were, indeed, thus occupied when Colonel Pedlar suddenly put his question. This was undoubtedly intended as a form of expressing polite interest in his colleague's day, rather than to show any very keen desire for further tactical information about the exercise, a subject with which Colonel Pedlar, and everyone else present, must by now be replete. However Colonel Hogbourne-Johnson chose to take the enquiry in the latter sense.

'Pretty bloody, Eric,' he said. 'Pretty bloody. If you want to know about it, read the sit-rep.'

'I've read it, Derrick.'

The assonance of the two colonels' forenames always imparted a certain whimsicality to their duologues.

'Read it again, Eric, read it again. I'd like you to. There are several points I want to bring up later.'

'Where is it, Derrick?'

Colonel Pedlar seemed to possess no intellectual equipment for explaining that he had absolutely no need, even less desire, to re-read the situation report. Perhaps, having embarked on the subject, he felt a duty to follow it up.

'Cocksidge will find it for you, Eric, writ in his own fair hand. Seek out the sit-rep, Jack.'

In certain moods, especially when he teased Widmerpool, the General was inclined to frame his sentences in a kind of Old English vernacular. Either because the style appealed equally to himself, or, more probably, because use of it implied compliment to the Divisional Commander, Colonel Hogbourne-Johnson also favoured this mode of speech. At his words, Cocksidge was on his feet in an instant, his features registering, as ever, deference felt for those of higher rank than himself. Cocksidge's demeanour to his superiors always recalled a phrase used by Odo Stevens when we had been on a course together at Aldershot:

'Good morning, Sergeant-Major, here's a sparrow for your cat.'

Cocksidge was, so to speak, in a chronic state of providing, at a higher level of rank, sparrows for sergeant-majors' cats. His own habitual incivility to subordinates was humdrum enough, but the imaginative lengths to which he would carry obsequiousness to superiors displayed something of genius. He took a keen delight in running errands for anyone a couple of ranks above himself, his subservience even to majors showing the essence of humility. He had made a close, almost scientific study of the likes and dislikes of Colonel Hogbourne-Johnson and Colonel Pedlar, while the General he treated with reverence in which there was even a touch of worship, of deification. In contact with General Liddament, so extreme was his respect that Cocksidge even abated a little professional boyishness of manner, otherwise such a prominent feature of his all-embracing servility, seeming by its appealing tone to ask forbearance for his own youth and immaturity. Widmerpool, to do him justice, despised Cocksidge, an attitude Cocksidge seemed positively to enjoy. The two colonels, on the other hand, undoubtedly approved his fervent attentions, appeared even appreciative of his exaggeratedly juvenile mannerisms. In addition, it had to be admitted Cocksidge did his job competently, apart from

37

such elaborations of his own personality. Now he came hurriedly forward with the situation report.

'Thanks, Jack,' said Colonel Pedlar.

He studied the paper, gazing at it with that earnest, apparently uncomprehending stare, of which Widmerpool had more than once complained.

'I've seen this,' he said. 'Seems all right, Derrick. Take it back where it belongs, Jack.'

'Glad it seems all right to you, Eric,' said Colonel Hogbourne-Johnson, 'because I rather flatter myself the operational staff, under my guidance, did a neat job.'

The bite in his tone should have conveyed warning. He terminated this comment, as was his habit, by giving a smirk, somehow audibly extruded from the left-hand side of his mouth, a kind of hiss, intended to underline the aptness or wit of his words. Unless in a bad humour he would always give vent to this muted sound after speaking. The fact was Colonel Hogbourne-Johnson did not attempt to conceal his own sense of superiority over a brother officer, inferior not only in appointment, regiment and mental equipment, but also in a field where Colonel Hogbourne-Johnson felt himself particularly to shine, that is to say in the arena where men of the world sparklingly perform. The play of his wit was often directed against the more leisurely intellect of Colonel Pedlar, whose efforts to keep up with all this parade of brilliance occasionally landed him in disaster. It was so on that night. After giving a glance at the situation report, he handed it back to Cocksidge, who received the document with bent head, as if at Communion or in the act of being entrusted with a relic of supreme holiness. There could be no doubt that the sit-rep had at least confirmed Colonel Pedlar in the belief that nothing remained to worry about where the exercise was concerned. At such moments as this one he was inclined to overreach himself.

'Going to finish up with a glass of port tonight, Derrick,' he asked, 'now that our exertions are almost at an end?'

'Port, Eric?'

A wealth of meaning attached to the tone given by Colonel Hogbourne-Johnson to the name of the wine. Widmerpool's mother, years before, had pronounced 'port' with a similar interrogative inflexion in her voice, though probably to imply her guests were lucky to get any port at all, rather than for the reasons impelling Colonel Hogbourne-Johnson so precisely to enunciate the word.

'Yes, Derrick?'

'Not tonight, Eric. Port don't do the liver any good. Not the sort of port we have in this Mess anyway. I shall steer clear of port myself, Eric, and I should advise you to do the same.'

'You do?'

'I do, Eric.'

'Well, I think I'll have a small glass nevertheless, Derrick. I'm sorry you won't be accompanying me.'

Colonel Pedlar gave the necessary order. Colonel Hogbourne-Johnson shook his head in disapproval. He was known to favour economy; it was said, even to the extent of parsimony. A glass of port was brought to the table. Colonel Pedlar, looking like an advertisement for some well known brand of the wine in question, held the glass to the lamp-light, turning the rim in his hand.

'Fellow in my regiment was telling me just before the war that his grandfather laid down a pipe of port for him to inherit on his twenty-first birthday,' he remarked.

Colonel Hogbourne-Johnson grunted. He did this in a manner to imply observation of that particular custom, even the social necessity of such a provision, was too well accepted in decent society for any casual commendation of the act to be required; though the tradition might be comparatively unfamiliar in what he was accustomed to describe as 'Heavy' infantry; and, it might be added, not much of a regiment at that.

'Twelve dozen bottles,' said Colonel Pedlar dreamily. 'Pretty good cellar for a lad when he comes of age.'

Colonel Hogbourne-Johnson suddenly showed attention. He began to bare a row of teeth under the biscuit-coloured bristles and small hooked nose.

'Twelve dozen, Eric?'

'That's it, isn't it, Derrick?'

Colonel Pedlar sounded nervous now, already aware no doubt that he had ventured too far in claiming knowledge of the world; had made, not for the first time, an elementary blunder.

'*Twelve dozen?*' repeated Colonel Hogbourne-Johnson.

He added additional emphasis to the question, carrying the implication that he himself must have misheard.

'Yes.'

'You're wide of the mark, Eric. Completely out of the picture.'

'I am, Derrick?'

'You certainly are, Eric.'

'What is a pipe then, Derrick? I'm not in the wine trade.'

'Don't have to be in the wine trade to know what a pipe of port is, old boy. Everyone ought to know that. Nothing to do with being a shopman. *More than fifty dozen*. That's a pipe. You're absolutely out in your calculations. Couldn't be more so. Mismanaged your slide-rule. Landed in an altogether incorrect map-square. Committed a real bloomer.

Got off on the wrong foot, as well as making a false start.'

'Is that a pipe, by Jove?'

'That's a pipe, Eric.'

'I got it wrong, Derrick.'

'You certainly did, Eric. You certainly got it wrong. You did, by Jove.'

'You've shaken me, Derrick. I'll have to do better next time.'

'You will, Eric, you will—or we won't know what to think of you.'

General Liddament seemed not to hear them. It was as if he had fallen into a cataleptic sleep or was under the influence of some potent drug. After this exchange between the two colonels, another long silence fell, one of those protracted abstinences from all conversation so characteristic of army Messes—British ones, at least—during which, as every moment passes, you feel someone is on the point of giving voice to a startling utterance, yet, for no particular reason, that utterance is always left pending, for ever choked back, incapable, from inner necessity, of being finally brought to birth. An old tin alarm-clock ticked away noisily on the dresser, emphasising the speedy passing of mortal life. Colonel Pedlar sipped away at his port, relish departed after his blunder. Cocksidge, with the side of his palm, very quietly scraped together several crumbs from the surface of the table cloth, depositing them humbly, though at the same time rather coyly, on his own empty plate, as if to give active expression, even in the sphere of food, to his perpetual dedication in keeping spick and span the surroundings of those set in authority over him, doing his poor best in making them as comfortable as possible. Only that morning, in the dim light at an early hour in the farmhouse kitchen, I had tripped over him, nearly fallen headlong, as he crouched on his knees before the fire, warming the butter ration so that its consistency might be appropriately emulsified for the General to slice with ease when he appeared at the breakfast table. No doubt, during all such silences as the one that now had fallen on the Mess, the mind of Cocksidge was perpetually afire with fresh projects for self-abasement before the powerful. By now there was no more to hope for, so far as food was concerned. It seemed time to withdraw from the board, in other respects unrewarding.

'May I go and see how the Defence Platoon is getting on, sir?'

General Liddament appeared not to have heard. Then, with an effort, he jerked himself from out of his deep contemplation. It was like asking permission from one of the supine bodies in an opium den. He took a few seconds more to come to, consider the question. When he spoke it was with almost biblical solemnity.

'Go, Jenkins, go. No officer of mine shall ever be hindered from attending to the needs of his men.'

A sergeant entered the room at that moment and approached the General.

'Just come through on the W/T, sir, enemy planes over the town again.'

'Right—take routine action.'

The sergeant retired. I followed him out into a narrow passage where my equipment hung from a hook. Then, buckling on belt and pouches, I made for the outbuildings. Most of the platoon were pretty comfortable in a loft piled high with straw, some of them snoring away. Sergeant Harmer was about to turn in himself, leaving things in the hands of Corporal Mantle. I ran through the matter of sentry duties. All was correct.

'Just come through they're over the town again, Sergeant.'

'Are they again, the buggers.'

Harmer, a middle-aged man with bushy eyebrows, largely built, rather slow, given to moralising, was in civilian life foreman in a steel works.

'We haven't got to wake up for them tonight.'

'It's good that, sir, besides you never know they won't get you.'

'True enough.'

'Ah, you don't, life's uncertain, no mistake. Here today, gone tomorrow. After my wife went to hospital last year the nurse met me, I asked how did the operation go, she didn't answer, said the doctor wanted a word, so I knew what he was going to say. Only the night before when I'd been with her she said "I think I'll get some new teeth". We can't none of us tell.'

'No, we can't.'

Even the first time I had been told the teeth story, I could think of no answer than that.

'I'll be getting some sleep. All's correct and Corporal Mantle will take over.'

'Good night, Sergeant.'

Corporal Mantle remained. He wanted to seize this opportunity for speaking a word in private about the snag arisen as to his candidature for a commission. Colonel Hogbourne-Johnson had decided to make things as difficult as possible. Mantle was a good NCO. Nobody wanted to lose him. Indeed, Colonel Hogbourne-Johnson had plans to promote him sergeant, eventually perhaps sergeant-major, when opportunity arose to get rid of Harmer, not young enough or capable of exceptional energy, even if he did the job adequately. Widmerpool, through whom such matters to some extent circulated, was not interested either way in

43

what happened to Mantle. He abetted Hogbourne-Johnson's obstructive tactics in that field, partly as line of least resistance, partly because he was himself never tired of repeating the undeniable truth that the army is an institution directed not towards the convenience of the individual, but to the production of the most effective organisation for an instrument designed to win wars.

'At the present moment there are plenty of young men at OCTUs who are potentially good officers,' Widmerpool said. 'Good corporals, on the other hand, are always hard to come by. That situation could easily change. If we get a lot of casualties, it *will* change so far as officers are concerned—though no doubt good corporals will be harder than ever to find. In the last resort, of course, officer material is naturally limited to the comparatively small minority who possess the required qualifications—and do not suppose for one moment that I presume that minority to come necessarily, even primarily, from the traditional officer class. On the contrary.'

'But Mantle doesn't come from what you call the traditional officer class. His father keeps a newspaper shop and he himself has some small job in local government.'

'That's as may be,' said Widmerpool, 'and more power to his elbow. Mantle's a good lad. At the same time I see no reason for treating Mantle's case with undue bustle. As I've said before, I have no great opinion of Hogbourne-Johnson's capabilities as a staff officer—on that particular point I find myself in agreement with the General—but Hogbourne-Johnson is within his rights, indeed perfectly correct, in trying to delay the departure of an NCO, if he feels the efficiency of these Headquarters will be thereby diminished.'

There the matter rested. Outside the barn I had a longish

44

talk with Mantle about his situation. By the time I returned to the house, everyone appeared to have gone to bed; at least the room in which we had eaten seemed at first deserted, although the oil lamp had not been extinguished. It had, however, been moved from the dinner table to the dresser standing on the right of the fireplace. Then, as I crossed the room to make for a flight of stairs on the far side, I saw General Liddament himself had not yet retired to his bedroom. He was sitting on a kitchen chair, his feet resting on another, while he read from a small blue book that had the air of being a pocket edition of some classic. As I passed he looked up.

'Good night, sir.'

'How goes the Defence Platoon?'

'All right, sir. Guards correct. Hay to sleep on.'

'Latrines?'

'Dug two lots, sir.'

'Down wind?'

'Both down wind, sir.'

The General nodded approvingly. He was rightly keen on sanitary discipline. His manner showed he retained the unusually good mood of before dinner. There could be no doubt the day's triumph over the Blue Force had pleased him. Then, suddenly, he raised the book he had been reading in the air, holding it at arm's length above his head. For a moment I thought he was going to hurl it at me. Instead, he waved the small volume backwards and forwards, its ribbon marker flying at one end.

'Book reader, aren't you?'

'Yes, sir.'

'What do you think of Trollope?'

'Never found him easy to read, sir.'

The last time I had discussed books with a general had

been with General Conyers, a much older man than General Liddament, one whose interests were known to range from psychoanalysis to comparative religion; and in many other directions too. Long experience of the world of courts and camps had given General Conyers easy tolerance for the opinions of others, literary as much as anything else. General Liddament, on the other hand, seemed to share none of that indulgence for those who did not equally enjoy his favourite authors. My answer had an incisive effect. He kicked the second chair away from him with such violence that it fell to the ground with a great clatter. Then he put his feet to the floor, screwing round his own chair so that he faced me.

'*You've never found Trollope easy to read?*'

'No, sir.'

He was clearly unable to credit my words. This was an unhappy situation. There was a long pause while he glared at me.

'Why not?' he asked at last.

He spoke very sternly. I tried to think of an answer. From the past, a few worn shreds of long forgotten literary criticism were just pliant enough to be patched hurriedly together in substitute for a more suitable garment to cover the dialectic nakedness of the statement just made.

'. . . the style . . . certain repetitive tricks of phrasing . . . psychology often unconvincing . . . sometimes downright dishonest in treating of individual relationships . . . women don't analyse their own predicaments as there represented . . . in fact, the author does more thinking than feeling . . . of course, possessor of enormous narrative gifts . . . marshalling material . . . all that amounting to genius . . . certain sense of character, even if stylised . . . and naturally as a picture of the times . . .'

46

'Rubbish,' said General Liddament.

He sounded very angry indeed. All the good humour brought about by the defeat of the Blue Force had been dissipated by a thoughtless expression of literary prejudice on my own part. It might have been wiser to have passed some noncommittal judgment. Possibly I should be put under arrest for holding such mutinous views. The General thought for a long time, perhaps pondering that question. Then he picked up the second chair from the floor where it had fallen on its side. He set it, carefully, quietly, at the right distance and angle in relation to himself. Once more he placed his feet on the seat. Giving a great sigh, he tilted back his own chair until its joints gave a loud crack. This physical relaxation seemed to infuse him with a greater, quite unexpected composure.

'All I can say is you miss a lot.'

He spoke mildly.

'So I've often been told, sir.'

'Whom do you like, if you don't like Trollope?'

For the moment, I could not remember the name of a single novelist, good or bad, in the whole history of literature. Who was there? Then, slowly, a few admired figures came to mind—Choderlos de Laclos—Lermontov—Svevo. . . . Somehow these did not have quite the right sound. The impression given was altogether too recondite, too eclectic. Seeking to nominate for favour an author not too dissimilar from Trollope in material and method of handling, at the same time in contrast with him—not only in being approved by myself—in possessing greater variety and range, the *Comédie Humaine* suddenly suggested itself.

'There's Balzac, sir.'

'*Balzac!*'

General Liddament roared the name. It was impossible

to know whether Balzac had been a very good answer or a very bad one. Nothing was left to be considered between. The violence of the exclamation indicated that beyond argument. The General brought the legs of the chair down level with the floor again. He thought for a moment. Fearing cross-examination, I began to try and recall the plots of all the Balzac books, by no means a large number in relation to the whole, I had ever read. However, the next question switched discussion away from the sphere of literary criticism as such.

'Read him in French?'

'I have, sir.'

'Get along all right?'

'I'm held up with occasional technical descriptions—how to run a provincial printing press economically on borrowed money, what makes the best roofing for a sheepcote in winter, that sort of thing. I usually have a fairly good grasp of the narrative.'

The General was no longer listening.

'You must be pretty bored with your present job,' he said.

He pronounced these words deliberately, as if he had given the matter much thought. I was so surprised that, before I could make any answer or comment, he had begun to speak again; now seeming to have lost all his former interest in writers and writing.

'When's your next leave due?'

'In a week's time, sir.'

'It is, by God?'

I gave the exact date, unable to imagine what might be coming next.

'Go through London?'

'Yes, sir.'

'And you'd like a change from what you're doing?

'I should, sir.'

It had never struck me that General Liddament might be sufficiently interested in the individuals making up Divisional Headquarters to have noticed any such thing. Certainly, as a general, he was exceptional enough in that respect. He was also, it occurred to me, acting in contrast with Widmerpool's often propagated doctrines regarding the individual in relation to the army. His next remark was even more staggering.

'You've been very patient with us here,' he said.

Again I could think of no reply. I was also not sure he was not teasing. In one sense, certainly he was; in another, he seemed to have some project in mind. This became more explicit.

'The point is,' he said, 'people like you may be more useful elsewhere.'

'Yes, sir.'

'It's not a personal matter.'

'No, sir.'

'We live such a short time in the world, it seems a pity not to do the jobs we're suited for.'

These sentences were closer to Widmerpool's views, though more sanely interpreted; their reminder that life was dust had a flavour, too, of Sergeant Harmer's philosophy.

'I'm going to send a signal to Finn.'

'Yes, sir.'

'Ever heard of Finn?'

'No, sir.'

'Finn was with me at the end of the last war—a civilian, of course—in the City in those days.'

'Yes, sir.'

General Liddament mentioned 'the City' with that faint touch of awe, a lowering of the voice, somewhere between reverence and horror, that regular soldiers, even exceptional ones like himself, are apt to show for such mysterious, necromantic means of keeping alive.

'But he put up a good show when he was with us.'

'Yes, sir.'

'An excellent show.'

'Yes, sir.'

'Got a VC.'

'I see, sir.'

'Then, after the war, Finn gave up the City. Went into the cosmetic business—in Paris.'

'Yes, sir.'

'Made a good thing out of it.'

'Yes, sir.'

'Now he's come back here with the Free French.'

'I see, sir.'

'I understand Finn's looking for suitable officers for the work he's doing. I suggest you drop in on him during your leave. Give him my compliments. Robin will issue you with an instruction when we get back to base.'

'Robin' was Greening, the ADC.

'Shall I mention this to the DAAG, sir?'

General Liddament thought for a moment. For a split second he looked as if he were going to smile. However, his mouth finally remained at its usual enigmatically set position when in repose.

'Keep it under your hat—keep it under your hat—just as well to keep it under your hat.'

Before I could thank him, or indeed any more might be said between us, the door of the room opened violently. Brigadier Hawkins, Commanding the Divisional artillery, came in almost at a run. Tall, lean, energetic, the CRA was the officer Widmerpool had commended for 'knowing how to behave when speaking on the telephone', in contrast with Colonel Hogbourne-Johnson. Widmerpool was right about that. Brigadier Hawkins, who had seen to it the Gunner Mess was the best run in the Division, was one of the few members of its staff who set about his duties with the 'gaiety', which, according to Dicky Umfraville, Marshal Lyautey regarded as the first requirement of an officer. Both Colonel Hogbourne-Johnson and Colonel Pedlar had to be admitted to fall unequivocally short in that respect. Not so, in his peculiar way, the General, whose old friend the Brigadier was said to be.

'Glad to find you still up, sir,' he said. 'Sorry to disturb you at this hour, but you should see a report at once they've just brought in. I thought I'd come myself, to cut out a lot of chat. The Blue Force we thought encircled is moving men in driblets across the canal.'

General Liddament once more kicked away the chair from his feet, sending it sliding across the room. He picked up a map-case lying beside him, and began to clear a space on the table, littered with a pipe, tobacco, other odds and ends. Trollope—I could not see which novel he had been reading—he slipped into the thigh pocket of his battle-dress. Brigadier Hawkins began to outline the situation. I made a move to retire from their conference together.

'Wait . . .' shouted the General.

He scribbled some notes on a pad, then pointed towards me with his finger.

'Wake Robin,' he said. 'Tell him to come down at once —before dressing. Then go and alert the Defence Platoon to move forthwith.'

I went quickly up the stairs to Greening's room. He was asleep. I shook him until he was more or less awake. Greening was used to that sort of thing. He jumped out of bed as if it were a positive pleasure to put an end to sleep, be on the move again. I gave him the General's orders, then returned to the Defence Platoon in the loft. They were considerably less willing than Greening to be disturbed. In fact there was a lot of grousing. Not long after that the Movement Order was issued. Advance Headquarters set off to a new location. This was the kind of thing General Liddament thoroughly enjoyed, unexpected circumstances that required immediate action. Possibly, in its minuscule way, my own case had suggested itself to him in some such terms.

'They do never want us to have no sleep,' said Sergeant-Major Harmer, 'but at least it's all on the way home.'

The Blue Force was held in check before the time limits of the exercise ran out. In short, the battle was won. It was nearly morning when Advance Headquarters were again ordered to move, this time in preparation for our return to base. We were on this occasion brought, contrary to habit in such manœuvres, into direct contact with our own Rear Headquarters; both branches of the staff being assembled together in a large farm building, cowshed or barn, waiting there while transport arrangements went forward. It was here that the episode took place which so radically altered Widmerpool's attitude towards Colonel Hogbourne-Johnson.

Cars and trucks were being marshalled along a secondary road on the other side of a ploughed field on which drizzle was falling. A short time earlier, a message had come through from base stating that the raid during the night had done damage that would affect normal administration on return to the town. Accordingly, Colonel Pedlar had driven back at once to arrange any modification of routine that might be required. Colonel Pedlar's presence with the rest of the staff could possibly, though by no means cer-

tainly, have provided a buffer between Widmerpool and
Colonel Hogbourne-Johnson. As things fell out, those two
came into direct impact just before we moved off. Widmerpool, with the two other officers who normally shared the
same staff car, was about to leave the cowshed where we
were hanging about, sleepless and yawning, when Colonel
Hogbourne-Johnson came suddenly through the doorway.
He was clearly very angry, altogether unable to control
the rage surging up within him. Even for a professionally
bad-tempered man, he was in a notably bad temper.
'Where's the DAAG?' he shouted at the top of his voice.

Widmerpool came forward with that serious, self-
important air of his, which, always giving inadequate
impression of his own capabilities, was often calculated to
provoke irritation in people he dealt with, even if not angry
already.

'Here I am, sir.'

Colonel Hogbourne-Johnson turned on Widmerpool as
if he were about to strike him.

'What the bloody hell do you think of yourself?' he
asked, still speaking very loudly.

'Sir?'

Widmerpool was not in the least prepared at that
moment for such an onslaught. Only a few minutes before
he had been congratulating himself aloud on how successfully had gone his share of the exercise. Now he stood
staring at Colonel Hogbourne-Johnson in a way that was
bound to make matters worse rather than better.

'Traffic circuits!' shouted Colonel Hogbourne-Johnson.
'What in God's name have you done about them? Don't
you know that's a DAAG's job? I suppose you don't.
You're not fit to organise an outing for a troop of Girl
Guides in the vicarage garden. Divisional Headquarters

53

has been ordered to move back to base forthwith. Are you aware of that?'

'Certainly, sir.'

'You've read the Movement Order? Have you got as far as that?'

'Of course, sir.'

'And made appropriate arrangements?'

'Yes, sir.'

'Then why is the Medium Field Regiment coming in at right angles across our route? That's not all. It has just been reported to me that Divisional Signals, and all their technical equipment, are being held up at another cross-roads half a mile up the same road by the Motor Ambulance Convoy making a loop and entering the main traffic artery just ahead of them.'

'I talked with the DAPM about distributory roads, sir—' began Widmerpool.

'I don't want to hear who you talked to,' said Colonel Hogbourne-Johnson, his voice rising quite high with fury. 'I want an immediate explanation of the infernal muddle your incompetence has made.'

If Widmerpool were not allowed to mention recommendations put forward by Keef, captain in command Military Police at Div HQ, also to some extent responsible for traffic control, it was obviously impossible for him to give a clear picture of what arrangements had been made for moving the column back. Brigadier Hawkins used to advocate two sovereign phrases for parrying dissatisfaction or awkward interrogation on the part of a superior: 'I don't know, sir, I'll find out', and its even more potent alternative: 'the officer/man in question has been transferred to another unit'. On this occasion, neither of those great international army formulae of exorcism were applicable. Mat-

54

ters were in any case too urgent. For once, those powerful twin spells were ineffective. However, Widmerpool, as it turned out, could do far better than fall back on such indecisive rubric, however magical, to defend his own position. He possessed chapter and verse. Instead of answering at once, he allowed Colonel Hogbourne-Johnson to fume, while he himself drew from the breast pocket of his battle-dress blouse a fat little notebook. After glancing for a second or two at one of its pages, he looked up again, and immediately began to recite a detailed account of troop movements, unit by unit, throughout the immediate area of Divisional activities.

'. . . Medium Field Regiment proceeding from . . . on the move at . . . must have reached . . . in fact, sir, should already have passed that point on the road twenty minutes ago . . . Motor Ambulance Convoy . . . shouldn't be anywhere near the Royal Signals route . . . proceeding to base via one of the minor roads parallel to and south of our main body . . . I'll show you on the map in a second, sir . . . only thing I can think of is some trouble must have occurred on that narrow iron bridge crossing the canal. That bridge wasn't built for heavy traffic. I'll send a DR right away . . .'

These details showed commendable knowledge of local transport conditions. Widmerpool recapitulated a lot more in the same vein, possessing apparently the movement-tables of the entire Division, an awareness that certainly did him credit as DAAG. The information should have satisfied Colonel Hogbourne-Johnson that, whatever else could have happened, Widmerpool, at least on the face of it, was not to blame for any muddle that might have taken place. However, Colonel Hogbourne-Johnson was in no state of mind to give consideration to any such possibility; nor, indeed, to look at the problem, or anything else, in the light of reason. There was something to be said for this approach. It is no good being too philosophical about such questions as a column of troops in a traffic jam. Action is required, not explanation. Such action may have to transcend reason. Historical instances would not be difficult to find. That concept provided vindication for Colonel Hogbourne-Johnson's method, hard otherwise to excuse.

'You've made a disgraceful mess of things,' he said. 'You ought to be ashamed of yourself. I know we have to put up these days with a lot of amateur staff officers who've had little or no experience, and possess even less capacity for learning the ABC of military affairs. Even so, we expect something better than this. Off you go now and find out immediately what's happened. When you've done so, report back to me. Look sharp about it.'

Widmerpool's face had gone dark red. It was an occasion as painful to watch as the time when Budd had hit him between the eyes full-pitch with an overripe banana; or that moment, even more portentous, when Barbara Goring poured sugar over his head at a ball. Under the impact of those episodes, Widmerpool's bearing had indicated, under its mortification, masochistic acceptance of the assault—'that slavish look' Peter Templer had noted on the day of the banana. Under Colonel Hogbourne-Johnson's tirade, Widmerpool's demeanour proclaimed no such thing. Perhaps that was simply because Hogbourne-Johnson was not of sufficiently high rank, in comparison with Budd (then captain of the Eleven), not a person of any but local and temporary importance in the eyes of someone like Widmerpool, who thought big—in terms of the Army Council and beyond—while Barbara had invoked a passion in him which placed masochism in love's special class. All the same, the difference is worth recording.

'Right, sir,' he said.

He saluted, turned smartly on his heel (rather in the manner of one of Bithel's boyhood heroes), and tramped out of the cowshed. Colonel Hogbourne-Johnson showered a hail of minor rebukes on several others present, then went off to raise hell elsewhere. In due course, not without delays, matters were sorted out. The dispatch-rider sent by Widmerpool returned with news that one of the field ambulances, skidding in mud churned up by the passing and repassing of tanks, had wedged its back wheels in a deep ditch. Meanwhile, the Light Aid Detachment, occupied some miles away with an infantry battalion's damaged carrier tracks, was not allowed—as too heavy in weight—to cross the iron bridge mentioned by Widmerpool. The LAD had therefore been forced to make a detour. The blocked road necessitated several other traffic diversions, which resulted in the temporary hold-up. That had already been cleared up by the time the DR reached the crossroads. No one was specially to blame, certainly not Widmerpool, such accidents as that of the ambulance representing normal wear-and-tear to be expected from movement of most of the available Command transport across country where roads were few and bad.

At the same time, to be unjustly hauled over the coals about such a matter is in the nature of things, certainly military things. Incidents like this must take place all the time in the army. In due course, I was to witness generals holding impressive appointments receiving a telling-off in the briskest manner imaginable, from generals of even greater eminence, all concerned astronomically removed from the humble world of Hogbourne-Johnson and Widmerpool. All the same, it was true Colonel Hogbourne-Johnson had been violent in his denunciation, conveying strictures on what he believed to be inefficiency with a kind of personal contempt that was unfitting, something over and above an official reprimand for supposed administrative mishandling. In addition, Hogbourne-Johnson, as a rule, seemed thoroughly satisfied with Widmerpool, as Widmerpool himself had often pointed out.

Whatever the rights and wrongs of the case, Widmerpool was very sore about it. He took it as badly as my former Company Commander, Rowland Gwatkin, used to take his tickings-off from the adjutant, Maelgwyn-Jones. In fact this comparatively trivial exchange between them transformed Widmerpool from an adherent of Colonel Hogbourne-Johnson—even if, in private, a condescending one—to becoming the Colonel's most implacable enemy. As it turned out, opportunity to make himself awkward arose the day we returned from the exercise. In fact, revenge was handed to Widmerpool, as it were, on a plate. This came about in connexion with Mr Diplock, Colonel Hogbourne-Johnson's chief clerk.

'Diplock may be an old rascal,' Colonel Hogbourne-Johnson himself had once commented, 'but he knows his job backwards.'

Repeating the remark later, Widmerpool had indulged in one of his rare excursions into sarcasm.

'We all know Diplock's a rascal,' he had remarked, 'and also knows his job backwards. The question is—does he know it forwards? In my own view, Diplock is one of the major impediments to the dynamic improvement of this formation.'

Mr Diplock (so styled from holding the rank of Warrant Officer, Class One) was a Regular Army Reservist, recalled to the colours at the outbreak of war. As indicating status bordering on the brink of a commissioned officer's (more highly paid than a subaltern), he was entitled to service dress of officer-type cloth (though high-collared) and shoes instead of boots. His woolly grey hair, short thick body, air of perpetual busyness, suggested an industrious gnome conscripted into the service of the army; a gnome who also liked to practise considerable malice against the race of men with whom he mingled, by making as complicated as possible every transaction they had to execute through himself. Diplock was totally encased in military obscurantism. Barker-Shaw, the FSO—as Bithel mentioned, a don in civil life—had cried out, in a moment of exasperation, that Diplock, with education behind him, could have taken on the whole of the Civil Service, collectively and individually, in manipulation of red tape; and emerged victorious. He would have outdone them all, Barker-Shaw said, in pedantic observance of regulation for its own sake to the detriment of practical requirement. Diplock's answer to such criticism was always the same: that no other way of handling the matter existed. Filling in forms, rendering 'states', the whole process of documentation, seemed to take the place of religion in his inner life. The skill he possessed in wielding army lore reached a pitch at which he could sabotage, or at least indefinitely protract, almost any matter that might have earned the disapproval of himself or any superior of whom he happened to be the partisan—in practice, Colonel Hogbourne-Johnson—while at the same time, if something administratively unusual had to be arranged, Diplock always said he knew how to arrange it. This self-confidence, on the whole justified, was perhaps the main reason why Colonel Hogbourne-Johnson was so well affected towards his chief clerk. The other was no doubt the parade of deference—of a deeper, better understood sort than Cocksidge's—that Diplock, in return, offered to

Colonel Hogbourne-Johnson. Diplock's methods had always irritated Widmerpool, although himself no enemy to formal routine as a rule.

'I told Hogbourne-Johnson in so many words this morning that we should never get anything done here so long as we had a chief clerk who was such an old woman. Do you know what he said?'

Although Widmerpool prided himself on his own grasp of army life, he had not been able wholly to jettison the more civilian approach, that you are paid to give advice to your superiors in whatever happens to be a specialised aspect of your particular job; that such advice should be presented in the plainest, most forceful terms. He never quite became accustomed to a tradition that aims at total self-effacement in the subordinate, more especially when his professional recommendations are controversial.

'What was the answer?'

'"Diplock wasn't an old woman when he won the Military Medal".'

'How does he know?—some old women are very tough.'

'I replied in the most respectful manner that Diplock won the MM a long time ago,' said Widmerpool, ignoring this facetiousness. 'That I was only referring to his present fumbling about with ACIs, Ten-Ninety-Eights, every other bit of bumph he can lay his hands on, especially when something is needed in a hurry. I suppose Hogbourne-Johnson thought he was snubbing me. He gave that curious snarling laugh of his.'

This slight brush had taken place before Widmerpool's more disastrous encounter with the Colonel. It illustrated not only Widmerpool's retention, in certain respects, of civilian values, but also his occasional lack of grasp of some quite obvious matter. Even in civilian life, a frontal attack would have been ill-judged in approaching a relationship in a business firm such as Hogbourne-Johnson's with Diplock. It was not going to alter the stranglehold Diplock enjoyed on Hogbourne-Johnson. At the same time, the fact that Widmerpool felt it possible to offer that remark about Diplock at all, absolved him from any suggestion of later deliberately assailing the Colonel through insidious attack by way of his own chief clerk. Widmerpool had already decided Diplock was unsatisfactory. When the time came, of course, he was not blind to pleasure derived from that method, but he did not contrive it of sheer malice. Once the ball was rolling, as DAAG, he had no alternative but to follow up suspicions aroused.

That even the lightest of such suspicions should have come into being on the subject of Mr Diplock behaving in an irregular manner might seem out of the question; far less, that there should be indications he was embezzling government funds. However, that was how things began to look. Possibly so much rectitude in observing the letter of the law in matters of daily routine required, psychologically speaking, release in another direction. General Conyers had been fond of expatiating on something of the sort. Anyway, the affair opened by Widmerpool saying one day, soon after the three-day exercise, that he was not satisfied with the financial administration of the HQ Sergeants' Mess.

'Something funny is going on there,' he said. 'Diplock is at the bottom of it, I'm sure. I've told those Mess treasurers time and again to take the bottle from the cellar account and charge it to the bar account. They never seem to understand. In Diplock's case, it looks to me as if he *won't* understand.'

These doubts were not set at rest as the weeks passed.

Not long after Widmerpool made this comment, several small sums of money disappeared from places where they had been deposited.

'I've recommended that cash-boxes be screwed to the floor,' said Widmerpool. 'At least you know then where they've been left. Diplock put all sorts of difficulties in the way, but I insisted.'

'Have you mentioned these losses higher up?'

'I had a word with Pedlar, who didn't at all agree with what I am beginning to wonder—I try to have as few direct dealings as possible now with Hogbourne-Johnson. I am well aware I should not receive a sympathetic hearing there. It will be a smack in the eye for him if my suspicions turn out to be correct.'

Then it appeared, in addition to the Sergeants' Mess, something unsatisfactory was afoot in connexion with the Commuted Ration Allowance.

'Mark my words,' said Widmerpool. 'This is all going to link up. What I require is evidence. As a start, you will go out to the Supply Column tomorrow and make a few enquiries. I must have facts and figures. As you are to be travelling in that direction, it will be a good opportunity to explain those instructions I have here just issued to RASC sub-units. You can go on to the Ammunition Company and the Petrol Company, after you've gathered the other information. Take haversack rations, as they're some distance apart, and the other thing will need some little time to extract. There may be lack of co-operation. CRASC has been difficult ever since the business of those trucks, which I was, in fact, putting to a perfectly legitimate use.'

At one time or another, Widmerpool had quarrelled with most of the officers at Divisional Headquarters. The row with CRASC—Commanding Royal Army Service Corps at

HQ, a lieutenant-colonel—had been about employment of government transport on some occasion when interpretation of regulations was in doubt. It had been a drawn battle, like that with Sunny Farebrother. Widmerpool's taste for conflict seemed to put him less at a disadvantage than might be supposed. His undoubted reputation for efficiency had indeed been to some extent built up on being regarded as a difficult man to deal with; rather than on much more deserved respect for the plodding away at unspectacular work to which he used to devote himself every night in his own office. Personal popularity is an asset easy to exaggerate in the transaction of practical affairs. Possibly it can even be a handicap. The fact that Widmerpool was brusque with everyone he met, even actively disobliging to most, never seemed in the last resort to weaken his position. However the Diplock affair was rather a different matter.

Enquiries at the quarters of the Supply Column indicated that, as Widmerpool supposed, all was not well. His feud with CRASC had certainly penetrated there, if unwillingness to spare time to impart information was anything to judge by. I left the place with a clearer understanding of my father's strictures, in the distant past, regarding Uncle Giles's transference to the Army Service Corps. However, certain essential details were now to some extent available. There could be no doubt that, at best, existing arrangements, so far as the Sergeants' Mess was concerned, were in disorder; at worst, something more serious was taking place in which Diplock might be involved. I brought back the material required by Widmerpool that evening.

'Just as I thought,' he said, 'I'll go and have a word with A & Q right away.'

Widmerpool stayed a long time with Colonel Pedlar. He had told me to wait until his return, in case further information collected during the day might be needed. When he came back to the room his ·expression immediately showed that he regarded the interview to have been unsatisfactory.

'Things will have to be looked into further,' he said. 'Pedlar's still unwilling to believe anything criminal is taking place. I don't agree with him. Just run through what they told you again.'

It was nearly dinner time when I arrived back that night at F Mess. I went to the bedroom to change into service dress. When I came down the stairs, the rest of them were going into the room where we ate.

'Buck up, Jenkins,' said Biggs, 'or you'll miss all the lovely bits of gristle Sopey's been collecting from the swill tubs all the afternoon for us to gnaw. Wonder he has the cheek to put the stuff he does in front of a man.'

He was in one of his noisy moods that night. When Biggs felt cheerful—which was not often—he liked to shout and indulge in horseplay. This usually took the form of ragging Soper, the Divisional Catering Officer. Soper, also a captain with '14–'18 ribbons, was short and bandy-legged, which, with heavy eyebrows and deep-set shifty eyes, gave him a simian appearance that for some reason suggested a professional comedian. In civil life one of the managers, on the supply side, of a chain of provincial restaurants, he was immersed in his work as DCO, never in fact making a remark that in the least fitted in with his promisingly slapstick appearance, or even one to be classed as a joke. Off duty he talked of scarcely any subject but army allowances. Biggs and Soper to some extent reproduced, at their lower level, the relationship of Colonel Hogbourne-Johnson and Colonel Pedlar in the General's Mess; that is to say they grated on each other's nerves, but, as twin veterans of the earlier war, maintained some sort of uneasy alliance. This bond was strengthened by a fellow feeling engendered by the relatively unexalted nature of their own appointments, both being much on their dignity where the 'G' staff—'operational' in duties—was concerned. There was, however, this important deviation in their reflection of the two colonels' relationship, for, although Biggs, aggressive and strident, so to speak bullied Soper (like Colonel Hogbourne-Johnson oppressing Colonel Pedlar), it was Soper who, vis-à-vis Biggs, enjoyed the role of man of the world, pundit of a wider sophistication. For example, Soper's knowingness about food—albeit army food—impressed Biggs, however unwillingly.

'How are the diet sheets, Sopey?' said Biggs, belching as he sat down. 'When are you going to give us a decent bit of beefsteak for a change? Can you tell me that?'

Soper showed little or no interest in this enquiry, certainly predominantly rhetorical in character. He had picked up a fork, from which he was removing with his thumbnail a speck of dried vegetable matter that adhered to the handle.

'Wouldn't you like to know,' was all he replied, adding to the table in general, 'Suppose if I complain about the washing up, we'll just be told there's not enough water.'

The raid that had taken place while we were on the Command exercise had damaged one of the local mains, so that F Mess was suffering from a water shortage; produced as excuse for every inadequacy in the kitchen.

'What do you say, Doc?' said Biggs, turning in the other direction. 'Couldn't you do with a nice cut of rump steak with a drop of blood on it? I know I could. Makes my mouth water, the thought. I'd just about gobble it up.'

Macfie, DADMS, a regular Royal Army Medical Corps

major, who had seen some pre-war service in India, gaunt, glum, ungenial, rarely spoke at meals or indeed at any other time. Now, glancing at Biggs with something like aversion, he made no answer beyond jerking his head slightly a couple of times before returning to the typewritten report he was thumbing over. No one among the two or three others at the table seemed any more disposed to comment.

'Come on, Doc, give the VD stats a rest at mealtimes,' said Biggs, who had perhaps drunk more beer than usual before dinner. 'God, I'm looking forward to some grub. Feel as empty as a bloody drum.'

He began stamping his feet loudly on the bare boards of the floor, at the same time banging with his clenched fists on the table.

'Buck up, waiter!' he shouted. 'When are we going to get something to eat, you slow bugger?'

'I want to swop night duty tomorrow,' said Soper. 'Take it on, Jenkins?'

'Mine's next Friday.'

'That'll do me.'

'They won't change the system again?'

'I'll act for you even if they do.'

'OK.'

Soper had caught me out once on a reorganised Duty Roster, avoiding my turn for night duty as well as his own. He was sharp on matters of that kind. I did not want to fall for a second confidence trick. Biggs ceased his tattoo on the surface of the table.

'Couldn't get a bloody staff car all day,' he said. 'I've a good mind to put in a report to A & Q.'

'Fat lot of good that would do,' said Soper.

He seemed satisfied now the fork was fairly clean, replacing it by the side of his plate. A spoon now attracted his attention.

'Organising that bloody boxing next week's going to be a bugger,' said Biggs. 'Don't have an easy life like you, Sopey, you old sod, driving round the units in state and tasting the sea-pie and Bisto. Hope this bloody beef isn't as tough tonight as it was yesterday. I'll be after you, Sopey, if it is. God, what a day it's been. A & Q on my tail all the time about that bloody boxing, and Colonel H-J giving me the hell of a rocket about a lot of training pamphlets I'd never heard of. He came through on the blower after I'd locked the safe and was looking forward to downing a pint. I'm just about brassed off, I can tell you. Went to see Bithel of the Mobile Laundry this afternoon. He's a funny bugger, if ever there was one. We had a pint together all the same. He soaks up that porter pretty easy. It was about one of his chaps that's done a bit of boxing. Might represent Div HQ, if he's the right weight. We could win that boxing compo, you know. That would put me right with Colonel H-J. Command's best welterweight had a bomb dropped on him in the blitz the other night, when they hit the barracks. Gives us a chance.'

Plates of meat were handed round by a waiter.

'Potatoes, sir?'

I was thinking of other things; thinking, to be precise, that I could do with a bottle of wine, then and there, however rough or sour. The Mess waiter was holding a dish towards me. I took a potato; then, for some reason, looked up at him. His enquiry, though quietly made, had penetrated incisively into these fantasies of the grape, cutting a neat channel, as it were, through both vinous daydreams and a powerful conversational ambience generated

67

by Biggs in his present mood. I glanced at the waiter's face for a second, then looked away, feeling, as I took a second potato, faintly, indeterminately uneasy. The soldier was tall and thin, about my own age apparently, with a pale, washed-out complexion, high forehead, dark hair receding at the temples and slightly greying. Bloodshot eyes, with dark, bluish rims, were alive, but gave at the same time an impression of poor health, this vitiated look increased by the fact of a battle-dress blouse with a collar too big in circumference for a long thin neck. I replaced the spoon in the potato dish, still aware of a certain inner discomfort. The waiter moved on to Biggs, who took four potatoes, examining each in turn, as, one after another, they rolled on to his plate, splashing gravy on the cloth. I followed the waiter with my eyes, while he offered the dish to Macfie.

'Spuds uneatable again,' said Biggs. 'Like bloody golf balls. They haven't been done long enough. That's all about it. Here, waiter, tell the chef, with my compliments, that he bloody well doesn't know how to cook water.'

'I will, sir.'

'And he can stick these spuds up his arse.'

'Yes, sir.'

'Repeat to him just what I've said.'

'Certainly, sir.'

'Where's he to stick the spuds?'

'Up his arse, sir.'

'Bugger off and tell him.'

So far as cooking potatoes went, I was wholly in agreement with Biggs. However, purely gastronomic considerations were submerged in confirmation of a preliminary impression; an impression upsetting, indeed horrifying, but correct. There could no longer be any doubt of that.

What I had instantaneously supposed, then dismissed as inconceivable, was, on closer examination, no longer to be denied. The waiter was Stringham. He was about to go through to the kitchen to deliver Biggs's message to the cook, when Soper stopped him.

'Half a tick,' said Soper. 'Who laid the table?'

'I did, sir.'

'Where's the salt?'

'I'll get some salt, sir.'

'Why didn't you put any salt out?'

'I'm afraid I forgot, sir.'

'Don't forget again.'

'I'll try not to, sir.'

'I didn't say try not to, I said don't.'

'I won't, sir.'

'Haven't they got any cruets in the Ritz?' said Biggs. 'Hand the pepper and salt round personally to all the guests, I suppose.'

'Mustard, sir—French, English, possibly some other more obscure brands—so far as I remember, sir, rather than salt and pepper,' said Stringham, 'but handing round the latter too could be a good idea.'

He went out of the room to find the salt, and tell the cook what Biggs thought about the cooking. Soper turned to Biggs. He was plainly glad of this opportunity to put the SOPT in his place.

'Don't show your ignorance, Biggy,' he said. 'Handing salt round at the Ritz. I ask you. You'll be going into the Savoy next for a plate of fish and chips or baked beans and a cup o' char.'

'That's no reason why we shouldn't have any salt here, is it?' said Biggs.

He spoke belligerently, disinclined for once to accept

Soper as social mentor, even where a matter so familiar to the DCO as restaurant administration was in question.

'Something wrong with that bloke,' he went on. 'Man's potty. You can see it. Hear what he said just now? Talks in that la-di-da voice. Why did he come to this Mess? What happened to Robbins? Robbins wasn't much to look at, but at least he knew you wanted salt.'

'Gone to hospital with rupture,' said Soper. 'This one's a replacement for Robbins. Can't be much worse, if you ask me.'

'This one'll have to be invalided too,' said Biggs. 'Only got to look at him to see that. Bet I'm right. No good having a lot of crazy buggers about, even as waiters. Got to get hold of blokes who are fit for something. Jesus, what an army.'

'Always a business finding a decent Mess waiter,' said Soper. 'Can't be picking and choosing all the time. Have to take what you're bloody well offered.'

'Don't like the look of this chap,' said Biggs. 'Gets me down, that awful pasty face. Can't stick it. Reckon he tosses off too much, that's what's wrong with him, I shouldn't wonder. You can always tell the type.'

From the rubber valve formed by pressure together of upper and lower lip, he unexpectedly ejected a small morsel of fat, discharging this particle with notable accuracy of aim on to the extreme margin of his plate, just beyond the potatoes left uneaten. It was a first-rate shot of its kind.

'When did the new waiter arrive?' I asked.

Nothing was to be gained by revealing previous acquaintance with Stringham.

'Started here at lunch today,' said Soper.

'I've run across him before,' said Biggs.

'At Div HQ?'

'One of the fatigue party fixing up the boxing ring,' said Biggs. 'Ever so grand the way he talks, you wouldn't believe. Needs taking down a peg or two in my opinion. That's why I asked him about the Ritz. Don't expect he's ever been inside the Ritz more than I have.'

Soper did not immediately comment. He stared thoughtfully at the scrap of meat rejected by Biggs, either to imply censure of too free and easy table manners, or, in official capacity as DCO, professionally assessing the nutritive value of that particular cube of fat—and its waste—in wartime. Macfie also gave Biggs a severe glance, rustling his typewritten report admonishingly, as he propped the sheets against the water jug, the better to absorb their contents while he ate.

'He'll do as a waiter so long as we keep him up to the mark,' said Soper, after a while. 'You're always grousing about something, Biggy. If it isn't one thing, it's another. Why don't you put a bloody sock in it?'

'There's enough to grouse about in this bloody Mess, isn't there?' said Biggs, his mouth full of beef and cabbage, but still determined to carry the war into Soper's country. 'Greens stewed in monkeys' pee and pepper as per usual.'

Stringham had returned by this time with the salt. Dinner proceeded along normal lines. Food, however unsatisfactorily cooked, always produced a calming effect on Biggs, so that his clamour gradually died down. Once I caught Stringham's eye, and thought he gave a faint smile to himself. Nothing much was said by anyone during the rest of the meal. It came to an end. We moved to the anteroom. Later, when preparing to return to the DAAG's office, I saw Stringham leave the house by the back door. He was accompanied by a squat, swarthy lance-corporal, no doubt the cook so violently stigmatised by Biggs. At Headquarters, when I got back there, Widmerpool was already in his room, going through a pile of papers. I told him about the appearance of Stringham in F Mess. He listened, showing increasing signs of uneasiness and irritation.

'Why on earth does Stringham want to come here?'

'Don't ask me.'

'He might easily prove a source of embarrassment if he gets into trouble.'

'There's no particular reason to suppose he'll get into trouble, is there? The embarrassment is for me, having him as a waiter in F Mess.'

'Stringham was a badly behaved boy at school,' said Widmerpool. 'You must remember that. You knew him much better than I did. He took to drink early in life, didn't he? I recall at least one very awkward incident when I myself had to put him to bed after he had had too much.'

'I was there too—but he is said to have been cured of drink.'

'You can never be sure with alcoholics.'

'Perhaps he could be fixed up with a better job.'

'But being a Mess waiter is one of the best jobs in the army,' said Widmerpool impatiently. 'It's not much inferior to sanitary lance-corporal. In that respect he has nothing whatever to grumble about.'

'So far as I know, he isn't grumbling. I only meant one might help in some way.'

'In what way?'

'I can't think at the moment. There must be something.'

'I have always been told,' said Widmerpool, '—and rightly told—that it is a great mistake in the army, or indeed elsewhere, to allow personal feelings about individuals to affect my conduct towards them professionally. I mentioned this to you before in connexion with

Corporal Mantle. Mind your own business is a golden rule for a staff officer.'

'But you're not minding your own business about who's to command the Recce Corps.'

'That is quite different,' said Widmerpool. 'In a sense the command of the Recce Corps *is* my business—though perhaps someone like yourself cannot see that. The point is this. Why should Stringham have some sort of preferential treatment just because you and I happen to have been at school with him? That is exactly what people complain about—and with good reason. You must be aware that such an attitude of mind—that certain persons have a right to a privileged existence—causes a lot of ill feeling among those less fortunately placed. War is a great opportunity for everyone to find his level. I am a major—you are a second-lieutenant—he is a private. I have no doubt that you and I will achieve promotion. So far as you are concerned, you will in any case receive a second pip automatically at the conclusion of eighteen months' service as an officer, which in your case cannot be far off by now. I think I can safely say that my own rank will not much longer be denoted by a mere crown. Of Stringham, I feel less certain. A private soldier he is, and, in my opinion, a private soldier he will remain.'

'All the more reason for trying to find him a suitable billet. It can't be much fun handing round the vegetables in F Mess twice a day.'

'We are not in the army to have fun, Nicholas.'

I accepted the rebuke, and said no more about Stringham. However, that night in bed, I reflected further on his arrival at Div HQ. We had not met for years; not since the party his mother had given for Moreland's symphony—where all the trouble had started about

Moreland and my sister-in-law, Priscilla. Priscilla, as it happened, was in the news once more, from the point of view of her family. Rumours were going round that, separated from Chips Lovell by the circumstances of war, she was not showing much discretion about her behaviour. A 'fighter-pilot' was said often to be seen with her, this figment, in another version, taking the form of a 'commando', loose use of the term to designate an individual, rather the unit's collective noun. However, all that was by the way. The last heard of Stringham himself had been from his sister, Flavia Wisebite, who had described her brother as cured of drink and serving in the army. At least the second of these two statements was now proved true. It was to be hoped the first was equally reliable. Meanwhile, there could be no doubt it was best to conceal the fact that we knew each other. Widmerpool also agreed on this point, when he himself brought up the subject again the following day. He too appeared to have pondered the matter during the night.

'So you think something else should be found for Stringham?' he asked that afternoon.

'I do.'

'I'll give my mind to it,' he said, speaking more soberly than on the earlier occasion. 'In the meantime, we are none of us called upon to do more than fulfil the duties of our respective ranks and appointments, vegetables or no vegetables. Now go and find out from the DAPM whether he has proceeded with the enquiries to be made in connexion with Diplock and his dealings. Get cracking. We can't talk about Stringham all day.'

So far as Stringham's employment in F Mess was concerned, nothing of note happened during the next day or two. On the whole he did what was required of him with competence—certainly better than Robbins—though he would sometimes unsmilingly raise his eyebrows when waiting on me personally. For one reason or another, circumstances always prevented speech between us. I began to think we might not be able to find an opportunity to talk together before I went on leave. Then one evening, on the way back to F Mess from Headquarters, I saw Stringham coming towards me in the twilight. He saluted, looking straight ahead of him, was going to pass on, when I put out a hand.

'Charles.'

'Hullo, Nick.'

'This is extraordinary.'

'What is?'

'Your turning up here.'

'What makes you think so?'

'Let's get off the main road.'

'If you like.'

We went down into a kind of alley-way, leading to a block of office buildings or factory works, now closed for the night.

'What's been happening to you, Charles?'

'As you see, I've become a waiter in F Mess. I always used to wonder what it felt like to be a waiter. Now I know with immense precision.'

'But how did it all come about?'

'How does anything come about in the army?'

'When did you join, for instance?'

'Too long ago to remember—right at the beginning of the Hundred Years War. After enlisting in my first gallant and glorious corps, and serving at their depot, I managed to exchange into the infantry, and got posted to this melancholy spot. You know how—to use a picturesque army phrase—one gets arsed around. I don't expect that happens any less as an officer. When the Royal Army Ordnance Corps took me to its stalwart bosom, I was not medically graded A.1.—which explains why in the past one's so often woken up feeling like the wrath of God—so I got drafted to Div HQ, a typical example of the odds and sods who fetch up at a place like that. Hearing there was a job going as waiter in F Mess, I applied in triplicate. My candidature was graciously confirmed by Captain Soper. That's the whole story.'

'But isn't—can't we find something better for you?'

'What sort of thing?'

That had been Widmerpool's question too. Stringham asked it without showing the smallest wish for change, only curiosity at what might be put forward.

'I don't know. I thought there might be something.'

'Don't you feel I'm quite up to the mark as waiter?' he said. 'Nick, you fill me with apprehension. Surely you are not on the side of Captain Biggs, who, I realise, does not care for my personality. I thought I was doing so well. I admit failure about the salt. I absolutely acknowledge the machine broke down at that point. All the same, such slips befall the most practised. I remember when the Duke of Connaught lunched with my former in-laws, the Bridgnorths, the butler, a retainer of many years' standing, no mere neophyte like myself, offered him macaroni cheese without having previously provided His Royal Highness with a plate to eat it off. I shall never forget my ex-father-in-law's face, richly tinted at the best of times—my late brother-in-law, Harrison Wisebite, used to say Lord Bridgnorth's complexion recalled Our Artist's Impression of the Hudson in the Fall. On that occasion it was more like the Dutch bulb fields in bloom. No, forget about the salt,

Nick. We all make mistakes. I shall improve with habit.'

'I don't mean——'

'Between you and me, Nick, I think I have it in me to make a first-class Mess waiter. The talent is there. It's just a question of developing latent ability. I never dreamed I possessed such potentialities. It's been marvellous to release them.'

'I know, but——'

'You don't like my style? You feel I lack polish?'

'I wasn't——'

'After all, you must agree it's preferable to hand Captain Biggs his food, and retire to the kitchen with Lance-Corporal Gwither, rather than sit with the Captain throughout the meal, to have to watch him masticate, day in day out. Gwither, on the other hand, is a delightful companion. He was a plasterer's mate before he joined the army, and, whatever Captain Biggs may say to the contrary, is rapidly learning to cook as an alternative. In addition to that, Nick, I understand you yourself work for our old schoolmate, Widmerpool. You're not going to try and swop jobs, are you? If so, it isn't on. How did your Widmerpool connexion come about, anyway?'

I explained my transference from battalion to Div HQ had been the result of Widmerpool applying for me by name as his assistant. Stringham listened, laughing from time to time.

'Look, Charles, let's fix up dinner one night. A Saturday, preferably, when most of the stuff at the DAAG's office has been cleared up after the week's exercise. We've a mass of things to talk about.'

'My dear boy, are you forgetting our difference in rank?'

'No one bothers about that off duty. How could they? London restaurants are packed with officers and Other

Ranks at the same table. Life would be impossible otherwise. My own brothers-in-law, for example, range from George, a major, to Hugo, a lance-bombardier. We needn't dine at the big hotel, such as it is, if you prefer a quieter place.'

'I didn't really mean that, Nick. I know perfectly well, in practice, we could dine together—even though you would probably have to pay, as I'm not particularly flush at the moment. It isn't that. I just don't feel like it. Dining with you would spoil the rhythm so far as I'm concerned. I wouldn't go so far as to say I'm actively enjoying what I'm doing at the moment—but then how little of one's life has ever been actively enjoyable. At the same time, what I'm doing is what I've chosen to do. Even what I want to do, if it comes to that. Up to a point it suits me. I've become awfully odd these days. Perhaps I always was odd. Anyway, that's beside the point. How I drone on about myself. Talking of your relations, though, I heard your brother-in-law, Robert Tolland, was killed.'

'Poor Robert. In the fighting round the Channel ports.'

'Awfully chic to be killed.'

'I suppose so.'

'Oh, yes, of course. You can't beat it. Smart as hell. Fell in action. I'm always struck by that phrase. Seems absolutely no chance of action here, unless Captain Biggs draws a gun on me for handing him the brussels sprouts the wrong side, or spilling gravy on that bald head of his. You know Robert Tolland was running round with my sister, Flavia, before he went to France and his doom. You never met Flavia, did you?'

'Saw her and Robert together when I was on leave last year.'

'Flavia never has any luck with husbands and lovers.

Think of being married to Cosmo Flitton and Harrison Wisebite in quick succession. Why, I'd make a better husband myself. No doubt you heard at the same time that my mother's parted company with Buster Foxe. She's having money troubles at the moment. One of the reasons why Buster packed up. I'm feeling the draught myself. Decided shortage of ready cash. My father left what halfpence he had to that French wife of his, supposing, quite mistakenly, Mama would always be in a position to shell out.'

'Your mother's at Glimber?'

'Good God, no. Glimber has some ministry evacuated there, so that's one problem off her hands. She's living in a labourer's cottage near a camp in Essex to be near Norman —you remember, her little dancer. At one moment she was getting up at half-past five every morning to cook his breakfast. There's devotion for you. Norman's going to an OCTU. Won't he look wonderful in a Sam Browne belt—that waist. Of course by the nature of things he can only be a son to her—a better son than her own, I fear— and in any case living with Norman in a cottage must be infinitely preferable to Buster in a castle, even allowing for the early rising. How sententious one gets. Just the sort of conclusion Tennyson was always coming to. You know, talking of the Victorians, I've taken to reading Browning.'

'Our General reads Trollope—the Victorians are obviously the fashion in this Division.'

'It was Tuffy who started me off on him. Rather a surprising taste for her in a way. You remember Tuffy? Nick, you make me talk of old times.'

'Miss Weedon—of course.'

'Tuffy cured me of the booze. Then, having done that,

she got bored with me. I see the point, there was nothing more to do. I mean I was going to prove absolutely impossible to set up as a serious member of civilised society. Stopping drinking alone was sufficient to ensure that. Even I myself grasped I'd become the most desperate of bores by being permanently sober. Then the war came along and I began to develop all sorts of martial ambitions. Tuffy didn't really approve of them, although the fact they were even within the bounds of possibility so far as I was concerned was a considerable tribute to herself. She saw, all the same, one way or another, I was going to escape her clutches. The long and the short of it was, I entered the army, while Tuffy married an octogenarian—perhaps by now even nonagenarian—general. Just the age when you get into your stride as a soldier. They'll probably appoint him CIGS.'

'You're out of touch. Generals are frightfully young nowadays. Widmerpool will be one at any moment. Anyway, they might do worse than employ General Conyers. I've known him for years.'

'My dear Nick, you know everybody. Not a social item escapes you. I myself can no longer keep up with births, marriages and deaths—well, deaths now and then perhaps, but not births and marriages. That's why being in the ranks suits me. No strain in that particular respect. Nobody asks you if you read in this morning's *Times* that so-and-so's engaged or somebody else is getting a divorce. All that had begun to get me down for some reason. Make me tired. Anyway, to hark back to the long and wearisome story of my own life, the point was that Tuffy, like everyone else, had had enough of me. She wanted another sphere in which to exercise her tireless remedial activities. That was why I took the shilling:

> I 'listed at home for a lancer,
> Oh who would not sleep with the brave?

I am not, as your familiarity with military insignia will already have proclaimed, strictly speaking a lancer—just as well, for these days I couldn't possibly take part in those musical rides lancers are always performing at the Military Tournament and places like that . . . haven't sat on a horse for years . . .'

Stringham paused a moment, beginning now to hum a bar or two of a jerky tune, the sort to which riders at a Horse Show might canter round the paddock.

> 'So-let-each-cavalier-who-loves-honour-and-me
> Come-follow-the-bonnets-of-Bonny-Dundee . . .'

He curled his wrists slightly, lifting them in the air as if holding reins. He seemed far away, to have forgotten completely that we were talking. I wondered how sane he remained. Then he came suddenly back to himself.

'. . . What was I saying? Oh, yes, A. E. Housman, of course . . . not my favourite poet, as a matter of fact, but that was just what happened . . . though I hasten to add I sleep with the brave only in the sense of dormitory accommodation. To tell the truth, Nick, I had the greatest difficulty in extracting the metaphorical shilling from an equally metaphorical Recruiting Sergeant. No magnificent figure with a bunch of ribbons in his cap, but several rather seedy characters in a stuffy office drinking cups of tea. Even so, they wouldn't look at me when I first breezed in. Then the war took a turn for the worse, in Norway and elsewhere, and they saw they'd need Stringham after all. One of the reasons I left the RAOC is that they have a peculiarly trying warrant rank called Conductor—just as if you were on a bus—so I made the exchange I spoke of. What a fascinating place the army is. Before I joined, I thought all you had to do when you fired a rifle was to get your eye and the sights and the target all in one line and then blaze away. The army has produced a whole book about it, a fat little volume. But my egotism is insufferable, Nick. Tell me about yourself. What have you been doing? How are you reacting to it all? You look a trifle harassed, if I may say so. Not surprising, working with Widmerpool.'

Stringham himself looked ill, though not in the least harassed.

'On top of everything else,' he said, 'one's getting frightfully old. Do you think I shall qualify as a Chelsea pensioner after the war? I'd like one of those red frockcoats, though I've never cared for Chelsea as a neighbourhood. No leanings whatever towards bohemian life. However, one may come to both before one's finished—residence in Chelsea and a bohemian to boot. You know I've been thinking a lot about myself lately, when scrubbing the floors and that sort of thing—an activity for some reason I often find myself quite enjoying—and I've come to the conclusion I'm narcissistic, mad about myself. That's why my marriage went wrong. I really was awfully glad when it was over.'

'Do you do anything about girls now?'

'Seem to have lost all interest. Isn't that strange? You know how it is. My great amusement now is trying to get things straight in my own mind. That takes me all my time, as you can imagine. The more I think, the less I know. Funny, isn't it? Talking of girls, what happened to our old pal, Peter Templer? Do you remember how he used to go on about girls?'

'Peter's said to have some government job to do with finance.'

'Not in the army?'

'Not so far as I know.'

'How like Peter. Always full of good sense, in his own way, though many people never guessed that at first. Married?'

'First wife ran away—second one, he appears to have driven mad.'

'Has he?' said Stringham. 'Well, I daresay I might have driven Peggy mad, had we not gone our separate ways. Talking of separate ways, I'll have to be getting back to my cosy barrack-room, or I'll be on a charge. It's late.'

'Won't you really dine one night?'

'No, Nick, no. Better not, on the whole. I won't salute, if you'll forgive such informality, as no one seems to be about. Nice to have had a talk.'

He moved away before there was time even to say good-night, walking quickly up the path leading to the main thoroughfare. I followed at less speed. By the time I reached the road at the top of the alley, Stringham was already out of sight in the gloom. I turned again in the direction of F Mess. This reunion with an old friend had been the reverse of enjoyable, indeed upsetting, painful to a degree. I tried to imagine what Stringham's present existence must be like, but could reconstruct in the mind only superficial aspects, those which least disturbed, probably even stimulated him. I felt more than ever glad a week's leave lay ahead of me, one of those curious escapes that in wartime punctuate army life, far more than a 'holiday', comparable rather with brief and magical entries into another incarnation.

Widmerpool did not like anyone going on leave, least of

all his own subordinates. In justice to this attitude, he appeared to treat his own leaves chiefly as opportunities for extending freedom of contact with persons who might further his military career, working scarcely less industriously than when on duty. I should be in no position to criticise him in that respect, if General Liddament fulfilled his promise in relation to this particular leave, during which I too hoped to better my own condition. However, it was probable the General had forgotten about his remarks during the exercise. The tactical upheaval which immediately followed our talk would certainly have justified that. I had begun to wonder whether I ought to remind him, and, if so, how this should be effected. However, by the morning after the encounter with Stringham, I had still taken no step in that direction; nor had I mentioned the meeting to Widmerpool, who was, as it happened, in a peevish mood.

'When do you begin this leave of yours?' he asked.

'Tomorrow.'

'I thought it was the day after.'

'Tomorrow.'

'If you see your relations, the Jeavonses, it's as well for you to know their sister-in-law staying as a paying guest in my mother's cottage wasn't a success. My mother decided she'd rather have evacuees.'

'Has she got evacuees?'

'She had some for a short time,' said Widmerpool, 'then they went back to London. They were absolutely ungrateful.'

He talked of his mother less than formerly, even giving an impression from time to time that Mrs Widmerpool's problems had begun to irritate him, that he felt she was becoming a millstone round his neck. Widmerpool had been on edge for several days past owing to the Diplock affair turning out to be so much more complicated than appeared on first examination. Diplock had brought all his own notable powers of causing confusion to bear, darkening the waters round him like a cuttlefish, so that evidence was hard to collect. Colonel Hogbourne-Johnson, for his part, made no secret of regarding Widmerpool's attempted impeachment of his chief clerk as nothing more nor less than a personal attack on himself. Indeed, Widmerpool could not have hit on a more wounding method of revenging himself on the Colonel, if his suspicions about Diplock were in due course to be substantiated. On the other hand, there was likely to be trouble if nothing more could be proved than that Diplock had been in the habit of keeping rather muddled accounts. Greening, the General's ADC, came into the DAAG's room at that moment. He handed me a small slip of paper.

'His Nibs says you know about this,' he said.

Greening, although he blushed easily, was otherwise totally unselfconscious. He was inclined to express himself in a curious, outdated schoolboy slang that sounded as if it had been picked up from some favourite book in childhood. Probably this habit appealed to General Liddament's taste for a touch of the exotic in his entourage. He may even have encouraged Greening in vagaries of speech, an extension of his own Old English. The piece of paper was inscribed with the typewritten words 'Major L. Finn, VC', followed by the name of a Territorial regiment and a telephone number. I saw I had underrated General Liddament's capacity for detail.

'Not much he forgets about,' said Greening, with artless curiosity. 'What is it?'

ADCs are a category of officer usually disparaged in

popular scrutiny of military matters. On the whole, they are no worse than most, better than many; while the job they do is the best possible training, if they are likely to rise in the world. Greening was, of course, not the sort likely to rise very far.

'Just a message to be delivered in London.'

Widmerpool looked up from the file in which he was writing away busily.

'What is that?'

'Something for the General.'

'What are you to do?'

'Telephone this officer.'

'What officer?'

'A Major Finn.'

'And say what?'

'Give him the General's compliments.'

'Nothing else?'

'See what he says.'

'Sounds odd.'

'That's what the General said.'

'Let me see.'

I handed him the paper.

'Finn?' he said. 'It's a Whitehall number.'

'So I see.'

'A VC.'

'Yes.'

'I seem to know the name—Finn. Sure I know it. When did the General tell you to do this?'

'On the last Command exercise.'

'At what moment?'

'After dinner on the last night.'

'Did he say anything else?'

'He talked about Trollope—and Balzac.'

86

'The authors?'

I was tempted to reply, 'No—the generals,' but discretion prevailed.

'You seem to be on very intimate terms with the Divisional Commander,' said Widmerpool sourly. 'Well, let me tell you that you will return from leave to find a pile of work. Are you waiting for something, Greening?'

'The General bade me discourse fair words to you, sir, anent traffic circuits.'

'What the hell do you mean?'

'I don't know, sir,' said Greening. 'That's exactly how the General put it.'

Widmerpool did not answer. Greening went away. He was one of the most agreeable officers at those Headquarters. I never saw him much except on exercises. Towards the end of the war, I heard, in a roundabout way, that, after return to his regiment, he had been badly wounded at Anzio as a company commander and—so my informant thought—might have died in hospital.

2

SULLEN REVERBERATIONS of one kind or another—blitz in England, withdrawal in Greece—had been providing the most recent noises-off in rehearsals that never seemed to end, breeding a wish that the billed performance would at last ring up its curtain, whatever form that took. However, the date of the opening night rested in hands other than our own; meanwhile nobody could doubt that more rehearsing, plenty more rehearsing, was going to be needed for a long time to come. Although these might be dispiriting thoughts, an overwhelming sense of content descended as the train reached the outskirts of London. Spring seas had been rough the night before, the railway carriage as usual overcrowded, while we threaded a sluggish passage through blackness towards the south; from time to time entering—pausing in—then vacating—areas where air-raid warnings prevailed. Viewed from the windows of the train, the deserted highways and gutted buildings of outlying districts created to the eye the semblance of an abandoned city. Nevertheless, I felt full of hope.

London contacts had to be sorted out. A letter from Chips Lovell, received only the day before, complicated an arrangement to dine with Moreland that evening. Lovell had heard I was coming on leave, and wanted to talk about 'family affairs'. That was a motive reasonable enough in principle; in practice, a disturbing phrase, when considered in relation to rumoured 'trouble' with Priscilla. Lovell was a Marine. He had been commissioned into the Corps at the time of its big expansion at the beginning of the war, soon after this being posted to a station on the East Coast. Evidently he had moved from there, because he gave a London telephone exchange (with extension) to find him, though no indication of what his new employment might be.

First, I called up the number Greening had consigned from General Liddament. The voice of Major Finn on the line was quiet and deep, persuasive yet firm. I began to tell my story. He cut me short at once, seeming already aware what was coming, another tribute to the General's powers of transmuting thought to action. Instructions were to report later in the day to an address in Westminster. This offered breathing space. A hundred matters of one sort or another had to be negotiated before going down to the country. After speaking with Major Finn, I rang Lovell.

'Look, Nick, I never thought you'd get in touch so soon,' he said, before there was even time to suggest anything. 'Owing to a new development, I'm booked for dinner tonight—first date for months—but that makes it even more important I see you. I'm caught up in work at lunch-time—only knocking off for about twenty minutes—but we can have a drink later. Can't we meet near wherever you're dining, as I shan't get away till seven at the earliest.'

'The Café Royal—with Hugh Moreland.'

'I'll be along as soon as I can.'

'Hugh said he'd turn up about eight.'

It seemed required to emphasise that, if Lovell stayed too long over our drink, he would encounter Moreland.

This notification was in Moreland's interest, rather than Lovell's. Lovell had never been worried by the former closeness of Priscilla and Moreland. Priscilla might or might not have told her husband the whole affair with Moreland had been fruitless enough, had never taken physical shape; if she had, Lovell might or might not have believed her. It was doubtful whether he greatly minded either way. I myself accepted they had never been to bed, because Moreland had told me that in one of his few rather emotional outbursts. It was because Moreland was sensitive, perhaps even touchy about such matters, that he might not want to meet Lovell. Besides, if Priscilla were now behaving in a manner to cause Lovell concern, he too might well prefer to remain unreminded of a former beau of his wife's; a man with whom he had in any case not much in common, apart from Priscilla. This turned out to be a wrong guess on my own part. Lovell showed no sign whatever of wanting to avoid Moreland. On the contrary, he was disappointed the three of us were not all dining together that evening.

'What a relief to meet someone like Hugh Moreland again,' he said. 'Pity I can't join the party. I can assure you it would be more fun than what faces me. Anyway, I'll go into *that* when we meet.'

Lovell was an odd mixture of realism and romanticism; more specifically, he was, like quite a lot of people, romantic about being a realist. If, for example, the suspicion ever crossed his mind that Priscilla had married him 'on the rebound', any possible pang would have been allayed, in his philosophy, by the thought that he had in the end himself 'got the girl'. He might also have argued, of course, that the operation of the rebound is unpredictable, some people thwarted in love, shifting, bodily and totally, on to another person the whole weight of a former strong emotion. Lovell was romantic, especially, in the sense of taking things at their face value—one of the qualities that made him a good journalist. It never struck him anyone could think or do anything but the perfectly obvious. This took the practical form of disinclination to believe in the reality of any matter not of a kind to be ventilated in the press. At the same time, although incapable of seeing life from an unobvious angle, Lovell was prepared, when necessary, to vary the viewpoint—provided obviousness remained unimpeded, one kind of obviousness simply taking the place of another. This relative flexibility was owed partly to his own species of realism—when his realism, so to speak, 'worked'—partly forced on him by another of his firm moral convictions: that every change which took place in life—personal—political—social—was both momentous and for ever; a system of opinion also stimulating to the practice of his profession.

Once Lovell's way of looking at the world was allowed, he could be subtle about ways and means. With the additional advantages of good looks and plenty of push, these methods were bringing fair success in his chosen career by the time war broke out. In marrying Priscilla, he had not, it is true, consummated a formerly voiced design to 'find a rich wife'; but then that project had never, in fact, assumed the smallest practical shape. Its verbal expression merely illustrated another facet of Lovell's romanticism—in this case, romanticism about money. He had, in any case, taken a keen interest in Priscilla even back in the days when he and I had been working on film scripts together (none of which ever appeared on any screen), so there was no surprise when the two of them married. At first he lost jobs and they were hard up. Priscilla, who had some taste for living dangerously, never seemed to mind these lean stretches. Lovell himself used to present an equally unruffled surface to the world where shortage of money was concerned, though underneath he certainly felt guilty regarding lack of it. He looked upon lack of money as a failing in himself; or, for that matter, in anyone else. From time to time, though without any strong force behind it, his romanticism would take moral or intellectual turns too. He would indulge, for instance, in fits of condemning material things and all who pursued them. These moods were sometimes accompanied by reading potted philosophies: the Wisdom of the East in one volume, Marx Without Tears, the Treasury of Great Thought. Like everyone else of his kind he was writing a play, an undertaking that progressed never further than the opening pages of the First Act.

'I never get time to settle down to serious writing,' he used to say, thereby making what almost amounted to a legal declaration in defining his own inclusion within an easily recognisable category of non-starting literary apprenticeship.

These were some of the thoughts about Lovell that passed through my head while I sat on a bench in the hall waiting to see Major Finn. The address in Westminster to which I had been told to report turned out to be a large house converted to the use of military headquarters. After a while a Free French corporal, his arm in a sling, joined me on the bench; then two members of the Free French women's service. Soon the three of them began an argument together in their own language. I re-read Moreland's postcard—a portrait of Wagner in a kind of tam-o'-shanter—confirming our dinner that night. Enigmatic in tone, its wording indefinably lacked the liveliness of manner usual in this, Moreland's habitual mode of communication.

We had not met since the first week of the war, soon after Matilda had left him. Matilda's subsequent marriage to Sir Magnus Donners had been effected with an avoidance of publicity remarkable even at a time when all sorts of changes, public and private, many of these revolutionary enough, were being quietly brought about. Muting the news of the ceremony was no doubt to some extent attributable to controls Sir Magnus found himself in a position to exercise in certain fields. The wedding of the divorced wife of a musician, well known even if not particularly prosperous, to a member of the Government rated in general more attention, even allowing for the paper shortage, than the few scattered paragraphs that appeared at the time. People said the break-up of Moreland's marriage had at first so much disturbed him that he seemed likely to go to pieces entirely, giving himself up increasingly to drink, while living as best he could from one day to the next. However, a paradox of that moment in the war was an excess, rather than deficiency, of musical employment; so that, in fact, Moreland found himself immersed in work of one sort or another, which, even if not very inspiring professionally, kept him alive and busy. That, at any rate, was what I had heard. Inevitably we had lost touch with each other since I had been in the army. Friendship, popularly represented as something simple and straightforward—in contrast with love—is perhaps no less complicated, requiring equally mysterious nourishment; like love, too, bearing also within its embryo inherent seeds of dissolution, something more fundamentally destructive, perhaps, than the mere passing of time,

93

the all-obliterating march of events which had, for example, come between Stringham and myself.

These rather sombre speculations were interrupted by a door opening nearby. A Free French officer in a képi appeared. Middle-aged, with spectacles, rather red in the face, he was followed from the room by a youngish, capless captain, wearing Intelligence Corps badges.

'Et maintenant, une dernière chose, mon Capitaine,' said the Frenchman, 'maintenant que nous en avons terminé avec l'affaire Szymanski. Le Colonel s'est arrangé avec certains membres du Commandement pour que quelques jeunes officiers soient placés dans le Génie. Il espère que vous n'y verrez pas d'inconvenient.'

'Vous n'avez pas utilisé la procédure habituelle, Lieutenant?'

'Mon Capitaine, le Colonel Michelet a pensé que pour une pareille broutille on pouvait se dispenser des voies hierarchiques.'

'Nous aurons des ennuis.'

'Le Colonel Michelet est convaincu qu'ils seront négligeables.'

'Ça m'étonnerait.'

'Vous croyez vraiment?'

'J'en suis sûr. Il nous faut immédiatement une liste de ces noms.'

'Très bien, mon Capitaine, vous les aurez.'

The English officer shook his head to express horror at what had been contemplated. They both laughed a lot.

'Au revoir, Lieutenant.'

'Au revoir, mon Capitaine.'

The Frenchman retired. The captain turned to me.

'Jenkins?'

'Yes.'

'Finn told me about you. Come in here, will you.'

I followed into his room, and sat opposite while he turned the pages of a file.

'What have you been doing since you joined the army?'

Reduced to narrative form, my military career up to date did not sound particularly impressive. However, the captain seemed satisfied. He nodded from time to time. His manner was friendly, more like the good-humoured approach of my old Battalion than the unforthcoming demeanour of most of the officers at Div HQ. The story came to an end.

'I see—how old are you?'

I revealed my age. He looked surprised that anyone could be so old.

'And what do you do in civilian life?'

I indicated literary activities.

'Oh, yes,' he said. 'I believe I read one.'

However, he showed none of General Liddament's keen interest in the art of the novel, made no effort to explore further this aspect of my life.

'What about French?'

It seemed simplest to furnish the same descriptive phrases offered to the General.

'I can read a book as a rule, but get held up with slang or something like the technical descriptions of Balzac.'

The captain laughed.

'Well,' he said, 'suppose we come back to that later. Are you married?'

'Yes.'

'Children?'

'One.'

'Prepared to go abroad?'

'Of course.'

95

'Sure?'

'Yes.'

He seemed almost surprised at this rather minimal acceptance of military obligation.

'We're looking for liaison officers with the Free French,' he said. 'At battalion level. They're not entirely easy to find. Speaking another language tolerably well seems so often to go with unsatisfactory habits.'

The captain smiled sadly, a little archly, across the desk at me.

'Whilst our Allies expect nothing less than one hundred per cent service,' he said, 'and quite right too.'

He fixed me with his eye.

'Care to take the job on?'

'Yes—but, as I explained, I'm no great master of the language.'

He did not reply. Instead, he opened a drawer of the desk from which he took a document. He handed this to me. Then he rose and went to a door on the other side of the room. It gave on to a smaller room, almost a cupboard, surrounded by dark green metal safes. In one corner was a little table on which stood a typewriter in its rubber cover. A chair was beside it.

'Make a French translation of these instructions,' he said. 'Subsistence Allowance is *frais d'alimentation*. Here is paper—and a typewriter, should you use one. Alternatively, here too is *la plume de ma tante*.'

Smiling not unkindly, he shut me in. I settled down to examine the printed sheet handed to me. It turned out to be an Army Form, one specifying current regulations governing issue, or non-issue, of rations to troops in the field. At first sight the prose did not seem to make much sense in English; I saw at once there was little hope of my own French improving it. Balzac on provincial type-setting was going to be nothing to this. However, I sat down and worked away, because I wanted the job badly.

Outside, on cornices and parapets of government buildings, starlings in thousands chattered and quarrelled. I was aware of that dazed feeling that is part of the impact of coming on leave. I read through the document again, trying to compose my mind to its meaning. This was like being 'kept in' at school. '. . . the items under (i) are obtainable on indent (A.B.55) which is the ordinary requisition of supplies . . . the items under (iii) and other items required to supplement the ration so as to provide variety and admit of the purchase of seasonable produce, and which are paid for with money provided by the Commuted Ration Allowance and Cash Allowance (iii above) . . . the officer i/c Supplies renders a return (A. F. B. 179), which shows the quantities and prices of rations actually issued in kind to the unit during the month, from which their total value is calculated . . .'

The instruction covered a couple of foolscap pages. I remembered being told never to write 'and which', but the mere grammar used by the author was by no means his most formidable side. It was not the words that were difficult. The words, on the whole, were fairly familiar. Giving them some sort of conviction in translation was the problem; conveying that particular tone sounded in official manifestos. Through the backwoods of this bureaucratic jungle, or the like, Widmerpool was hunting down Mr Diplock, in relentless safari. Such distracting thoughts had to be put from the mind. I chose *la plume de ma tante* in preference to the typewriter, typescript imparting an awful bareness to language of any kind, even one's own. For a time I sweated away. Some sort of a version at last appeared. I read it through several times, making corrections. It did not sound ideally idiomatic French; but then the original did not sound exactly idiomatic English. After embodying a few final improvements, I opened the door a crack.

'Come in, come in,' said the captain. 'Have you finished? I thought you might have succumbed. It's dreadfully stuffy in there.'

He was sitting with another officer, also a captain, tall, fair, rather elegant. A blue fore-and-aft cap lay beside him with the lion-and-unicorn General Service badge. I passed my translation across the desk to the I. Corps captain. He took it, and, rising from his chair, turned to the other man.

'I'll be back in a moment, David,' he said—and to me: 'Take a seat while I show this to Finn.'

He went out of the room. The other officer nodded to me and laughed. It was Pennistone. We had met on a train during an earlier leave of mine and had talked of Vigny. We had talked of all sorts of other things, too, that seemed to have passed out of my life for a long time. I remembered now Pennistone had insisted his own military employments were unusual. No doubt the Headquarters in which I now found myself represented the sort of world in which he habitually functioned.

'Splendid,' he said. 'Of course we agreed to meet as an exercise of the will. I'm ashamed to say I'd forgotten until now. Your own moral determination does you credit. I congratulate you. Or is it just one of those eternal recurrences of Nietzsche, which one gets so used to? Have you come to work here?'

I explained the reason for my presence in the building.

'So you may be joining the Free Frogs.'

'And you?'

'I look after the Poles.'

'Do they have a place like this too?'

'Oh, no. The Poles are dealt with as a Power. They have an ambassador, a military attaché, all that. The point about France is that we still recognise the Vichy Government. The other Allied Governments are those in exile over here in London. That is why the Free French have their own special mission.'

'You've just come to see them?'

'To discuss some odds and ends of Polish affairs that overlap with Free French matters.'

We talked for a while. The other captain returned.

'Finn wants to see you,' he said.

I followed him along the passage into a room where an officer was sitting behind a desk covered with papers. The I. Corps captain announced my name and withdrew. I had left my cap in the other office, so, on entering, could not salute, but, with the formality that prevailed in the area where I was serving, came to attention. The major behind the desk seemed surprised at this. He rose very slowly from his desk, and, keeping his eye on me all the time, came round to the front and shook hands. He was small, cleanshaved, almost square in shape, with immensely broad shoulders, large head, ivory-coloured face, huge nose. His grey eyes were set deep back in their sockets. He looked like an enormous bird, an ornithological specimen very different from Colonel Hogbourne-Johnson, kindly but at the same time immensely more powerful. I judged him in his middle fifties. He wore an old leather-buttoned service-dress tunic, with a VC, Légion d'Honneur, Croix de Guerre avec palmes, and a couple of other foreign decorations I could not identify.

'Sit down, Jenkins,' he said.

He spoke quietly, almost whispered. I sat down. He began to fumble among his papers.

'I had a note from your Divisional Commander,' he said. 'Where is it? Draw that chair a bit nearer. I'm rather deaf in this ear. How is General Liddament?'

'Very well, sir.'

'Knocking the Division into shape?'

'That's it, sir.'

'Territorial Division, isn't it?'

'Yes, sir.'

'He'll get a Corps soon.'

'You think so, sir?'

Major Finn nodded. He seemed a little embarrassed about something. Although he gave out an extraordinary sense of his own physical strength and endurance, there was also something mild, gentle, almost undecided, about his manner.

'You know why you've been sent here?' he asked.

'It was explained, sir.'

He lowered his eyes to what I now saw was my translation. He began to read it to himself, his lips moving faintly. After a line or two of doing this, it became clear to me what the answer was going to be. The only question that remained was how long the agony would be drawn out. Major Finn read the whole of my version through to himself; then, rather nobly, read it through again. This was either to give dramatic effect, or to rouse himself to the required state of tension for making an unwelcome announcement. Those, at least, were the reasons that occurred to me at the time, because he must almost certainly have gone through the piece when the captain had first brought it to him. I appreciated the gesture, which indicated he was doing the best he could for me, including not sparing himself. When he came to the end for the second time, he looked across the desk, and, shaking his head, sighed and smiled.

'Well . . .' he said.

I was silent.

'Won't do, I'm afraid.'

'No, sir?'

'Not as your written French stands.'

He took up a pencil and tapped it on the desk.

'We'd have liked to have you . . .'

'Yes, sir.'

'Masham agrees.'

'Masham' I took to be the I. Corps captain.

'But this translation . . .'

He spoke for a second as if I might have intended a deliberate insult to himself and his uniform by the botch I had made of it, but that he was prepared magnanimously to overlook that. Then, as if regretting what might have appeared momentary unkindness, in spite of my behaviour, he rose and shook hands again, gazing into the middle distance of the room. The vision to be seen there was certainly one of total failure.

'. . . not sufficiently accurate.'

'No, sir.'

'In fact, doesn't begin to be.'

'I see, sir.'

'You understand me?'

'Of course, sir.'

'A pity.'

We stared at each other.

'Otherwise I think you would have done us well.'

Major Finn paused. He appeared to consider this

hypothesis for a long time. There did not seem much more to be said. I hoped the interview would end as quickly as possible.

'Perfectly suitable . . .' he repeated.

His voice was far away now. There was another long pause. Then a thought struck him. His face lighted up.

'Perhaps it's only written French you're shaky in.'

He wrinkled his broad, ivory-coloured forehead.

'Now let us postulate the 9th Regiment of Colonial Infantry are on the point of mutiny,' he said. 'They may be prepared to abandon Vichy and come over to the Allies. How would you harangue them?'

'In French, sir?'

'Yes, in French.'

He spoke eagerly, as if he expected something enjoyably dramatic.

'I'm afraid I should have to fall back on English, sir.'

His face fell again.

'I feared that,' he said.

Failure was certainly total. I had been given a second chance, had equally bogged it. Major Finn stroked the enormous bumpy contours of his nose.

'Look here,' he said, 'I'll tell you what I'll do. I'll make a note of your name.'

'Yes, sir?'

'There may be certain changes taking place in the near future. Not here, elsewhere. But don't count on it. That's the best I can say. I don't question anything General Liddament suggests. It's just the language.'

'Thank you, sir.'

He smiled.

'You're on leave, aren't you?'

'Yes, sir.'

'Wouldn't mind some leave myself.'

'No, sir?'

'And my respects to General Liddament.'

'I'll convey them, sir.'

'A great man.'

I made a suitable face and left the room, disappointed and furious with myself. The fact that such an eventuality was in some degree to be expected made things no better. To have anyone in the army—let alone a general—show interest in your individual career is a rare enough experience. To fall at the language hurdle—just the field in which someone like myself, anyway in the eyes of General Liddament, might be expected to show reasonable proficiency—seemed to let down the General too. There would be little hope of his soliciting further candidatures in my interest. Why should he? I wondered why I had never taken the trouble in the past to learn French properly; as a boy, for instance, staying with the Leroys at La Grenadière, or in the course of innumerable other opportunities. At the same time, I was aware that a liaison officer at battalion level would be required to show considerable fluency. Perhaps it was just Fate. As for having a note made of my name, that was to be regarded as a polite formula on the part of Major Finn—an unusually likeable man—an echo of civilian courtesies from someone who took a pride in possessing good manners as well as a VC; a gesture to be totally disregarded for all practical purposes.

I returned to the captain's room. Pennistone was still there. He was about to leave, standing up, wearing his cap.

'Well then,' he was saying. 'On the first of next month Szymanski ceases to serve under the Free French authority, and comes under the command of the Polish Forces in Great Britain. That's settled at last.'

Masham, the I. Corps captain, turned to me. I explained the deal was off. He knew, of course, already.

'Sorry,' he said. 'Thanks for looking in. I hear you and David know each other.'

After taking leave of him, Pennistone and I went out together into the street. He asked what had happened. I outlined the interview with Major Finn. Pennistone listened with attention.

'Finn seems to have been well disposed towards you,' he said.

'I liked him—what's his story?'

'Some fantastic episode in the first war, when he got his VC. After coming out of the army, he decided to go into the cosmetics business—scent, face powder, things like that, the last trade you'd connect him with. He talks very accurate French with the most outlandish accent you ever heard. He's been a great success with the Free French— liked by de Gaulle, which is not everyone's luck.'

'Surprising he's not got higher rank.'

'Finn could have become a colonel half-a-dozen times over since rejoining the army,' said Pennistone. 'He always says he prefers not to have too much responsibility. He has his VC, which always entails respect—and which he loves talking about. However, I think he may be tempted at last to accept higher rank.'

'To what?'

'Very much in the air at the moment. All I can say is, you may be more likely to hear from him than you think.'

'Does he make money at his cosmetics?'

'Enough to keep a wife and daughter hidden away somewhere.'

'Why are they hidden away?'

'I don't know,' said Pennistone, laughing. 'They just are. There are all kinds of things about Finn that are not explained. Keeping them hidden away is part of the Finn system. When I knew him in Paris, I soon found he had a secretive side.'

'You knew him before the war?'

'I came across him, oddly enough, when I was in textiles, working over there.'

'Textiles are your job?'

'I got out in the end.'

'Into what?'

Pennistone laughed again, as if that were an absurd question to ask.

'Oh, nothing much really,' he said. 'I travel about a lot —or used to before the war. I think I told you, when we last met, that I'm trying to write something about Descartes.'

All this suggested—as it turned out rightly—that Pennistone, as well as Finn, had his secretive side. When I came to know him better, I found what mattered to Pennistone was what went on in his head. He could rarely tell you what he had done in the past, or proposed to do in the future, beyond giving a bare statement of places he had visited or wanted to visit, books he had read or wanted to read. On the other hand, he was able to describe pretty lucidly what he had thought—philosophically speaking— at any given period of his life. While other people lived for money, power, women, the arts, domesticity, Pennistone liked merely thinking about things, arranging his mind. Nothing else ever seemed to matter to him. It was the aim Stringham had announced now as his own, though Pennistone was a very different sort of person from

Stringham, and better equipped for perfecting the process. I only found out these things about him at a later stage.

'Give me the essential details regarding yourself,' Pennistone said. 'Unit, army number, that sort of thing—just in case anything should crop up where I myself might be of use.'

I wrote it all down. We parted company, agreeing that Nietzschean Eternal Recurrences must bring us together soon again.

Even by the time I reached the Café Royal that evening, I was still feeling humiliated by the failure of the Finn interview. The afternoon had been devoted to odd jobs, on the whole tedious. The tables and banquettes of the large tasteless room looked unfamiliar occupied by figures in uniform. There was no one there I had ever seen before. I sat down and waited. Lovell did not arrive until nearly half-past seven. He wore captain's pips. It was hard not to labour under a sense of being left behind in the military race. I offered congratulations.

'You don't get into the really big money until you're a major,' he said. 'That should be one's aim.'

'Vaulting ambition.'

'Insatiable.'

'Where do you function?'

'Headquarters of Combined Operations,' he said, 'that curious toy fort halfway down Whitehall. It's a great place for Royal Marines. A bit of luck your being on leave, Nick. One or two things I want to talk about. First of all, will you agree to be executor of my will?'

'Of course.'

'Perfectly simple. Whatever there is—which isn't much, I can assure you—goes to Priscilla, then to Caroline.'

'That doesn't sound too complicated.'

One never knows what may happen to one.'

'No, indeed.'

The remark echoed Sergeant Harmer's views. There was a pause. I had the sudden sense that Lovell was going to broach some subject I should not like. This apprehension turned out to be correct.

'Another small matter,' he said.

'Yes?'

'It would interest me to hear more of this fellow Stevens. You seem to be mainly responsible for bringing him into our lives, Nick.'

'If you mean someone called Odo Stevens, he and I were on a course together at Aldershot about a year ago. I didn't know he was in our lives. He isn't in mine. I haven't set eyes on him since then.'

I had scarcely thought of Stevens since he had been expelled from the course. Now the picture of him came back forcibly. Lovell's tone was not reassuring. It was possible to guess something of what might be happening.

'You introduced him into the family,' said Lovell.

He spoke calmly, not at all accusingly, but I recognised in his eye the intention to stage a dramatic announcement.

'One weekend leave from Aldershot Stevens gave me a lift in his very brokendown car as far as Frederica's. Then he took me back on Sunday night. Isobel was staying there. It was just before she had her baby. In fact, the birth started that night. Stevens got RTU-ed soon after we got back on the course. I haven't seen or heard of him since.'

'You haven't?'

'Not a word.'

'Priscilla was at Frederica's then.'

'I remember.'

'She met Stevens.'

'She must have done.'

'She's been with him lately up in a hotel in Scotland,' said Lovell, 'living more or less openly, so there's no point in not mentioning it.'

There was nothing to be said to that. Stevens had certainly struck up some sort of an acquaintance with Priscilla on that occasion at Frederica's. I could recall more. Some question of getting a piece of jewellery mended for her had arisen. Such additional consequences as Lovell outlined were scarcely to be foreseen when I took Stevens to the house. Nevertheless, it was an unfortunate introduction. However, this merely confirmed stories going round. No doubt Stevens, by now, was a figure with some sort of war career behind him. That could happen in the matter of a few weeks. That Stevens might be the 'commando', or whatever shape Priscilla's alleged fancy-man took, had never suggested itself to me. Lovell lit a cigarette. He puffed out a cloud of smoke. His evident inclination to adopt a stylised approach—telling the story as we might have tried to work it out together in a film script years before—was some alleviation of immediate embarrassments caused by the disclosure. The dramatic manner he had assumed accorded with his own conception of how life should be lived. I was grateful for it. By this means things were made easier.

'When did all this start?'

'Pretty soon after they first met.'

'I see.'

'I was down at that godforsaken place on the East Coast. There was nowhere near for her to live. It wasn't my fault we weren't together.'

'Is Stevens stationed in Scotland?'

'So far as I know. He did rather well somewhere—was

it the Lofoten raid? That sort of thing. He's a hero on top of everything else. I suppose if I were to do something where I could get killed, instead of composing lists of signal equipment and suchlike, I might make a more interesting husband.'

'I don't think so for a moment.'

In giving this answer, I spoke a decided opinion. To assume such a thing was a typical instance of Lovell's taste, mentioned earlier, for the obvious. It was a supposition bound to lead to a whole host of erroneous conclusions—that was how the conjecture struck me—regarding his own, or anyone else's, married life.

'You may be right,' he said.

He spoke as if rather relieved.

'Look at it the other way. Think of all the heroes who had trouble with their wives.'

'Who?'

'Agamemnon, for instance.'

'Well, that caused enough dislocation,' said Lovell. 'What's Stevens like, apart from his heroism?'

'In appearance?'

'Everything about him.'

'Youngish, comes from Birmingham, traveller in costume jewellery, spot of journalism, good at languages, short, thickset, very fair hair, easy to get on with, keen on the girls.'

'Sounds not unlike me,' said Lovell, 'except that up to date I've never travelled in costume jewellery—and I still rather pride myself on my figure.'

'There is a touch of you about him, Chips. I thought so at Aldershot.'

'You flatter me. Anyway, he seems more of a success than I am with my own wife. If he is keen on the girls, I suppose making for Priscilla would be a matter of routine?'

'So I should imagine.'

'You liked him?'

'We got on pretty well.'

'Why was he Returned-to-Unit?'

'For cutting a lecture.'

Lovell seemed all at once to lose interest in Stevens and his personality. His manner changed. There could be no doubt he was very upset.

'So far as I can see there was nothing particularly wrong with our marriage,' he said. 'If I hadn't been sent to that God-awful spot, it would have gone on all right. At least that's how things appeared to me. I don't particularly want a divorce even now.'

'Is there any question of a divorce?'

'It isn't going to be much fun living with a woman who's in love with someone else.'

'Lots of people do it, and *vice versa*.'

'At best, it's never going to be the same.'

'Nothing ever remains the same. Marriage or anything else.'

'I thought your theory was that everything did always remain the same?'

'Everything alters, yet does remain the same. It might even improve matters.'

'Do you really think so?'

'Not really.'

'Neither do I,' said Lovell, 'though I see what you mean. That's if she's prepared to come back and live with me. I'm not even sure of that. I think she wants to marry Stevens.'

'She must be mad.'

'Mad she may be, but that's the way she's talking.'

'Where's Caroline?'

'My parents are looking after her.'

'And Priscilla herself?'

'Staying with Molly Jeavons—though I only found out that by chance yesterday. She's been moving about among various relations, is naturally at times rather vague about her whereabouts, so far as keeping me informed is concerned.'

'You've dished all this up with her?'

'On my last leave—making it a charming affair.'

'But lately?'

'Since then, we've been out of touch more than once. We are at this moment, until I found, quite by chance, she was at the Jeavonses'. I'm hoping to see her tonight. That's why I can't dine with you.'

'You and Priscilla are dining together?'

'Not exactly. You remember Bijou Ardglass, that gorgeous mannequin, one-time girl-friend of Prince Theodoric? I ran into her yesterday on my way to Combined Ops. She's driving for the Belgians or Poles, one of the Allied contingents—an odd female organisation run by Lady McReith, whom Bijou was full of stories about. Bijou asked me to a small party she is giving for her fortieth birthday, about half-a-dozen old friends at the Madrid.'

'Bijou Ardglass's fortieth birthday.'

'Makes you think.'

'I only knew her by sight, but even so—and Priscilla will be there?'

'Bijou found her at Aunt Molly's. Of course Priscilla told Bijou I was on the East Coast. I was when we last exchanged letters. I explained to Bijou I'd just been posted to London at short notice—which was quite true—and hadn't managed to get together with Priscilla yet.'

'You haven't called up Priscilla at the Jeavonses'?'

'I thought it would be best if we met at Bijou's party—without Priscilla knowing I was going to be there. I have a reason for that. The Madrid was the place we celebrated our engagement. The Madrid might also be the place where we straightened things out.'

That was just like Lovell. Everything had to be staged. Perhaps he was right, and everything does have to be staged. That is a system that can at least be argued as the best. At any rate, people must run their lives on their own terms.

'I mean it's worth making an effort to patch things up,' he said, 'don't you think, Nick?'

He asked the question as if he had no idea what the answer would be, possibly even expecting a negative rather than affirmative one.

'Yes, of course—every possible effort.'

'You can imagine what all this is like going on in one's head, round and round for ever, while you're trying to sort out a lot of bloody stuff about radios and landing-craft. For instance, if she goes off with Stevens, think of all the negotiations about Caroline, all that kind of thing.'

'Chips—Hugh Moreland has appeared at the door on the other side of the room. Is there anything else you want to say that's urgent?'

'Nothing. I've got it all off my chest now. That was what I needed. You understand?'

'Of course.'

'The point is, you agree it's worth taking trouble to get on an even keel again?'

'Can't say it too strongly.'

Lovell nodded several times.

'And you'll be my executor?'

'Honoured.'

'I'll write to the solicitors then. Marvellous to have got that fixed. Hullo, Hugh, how are you? Ages since we met.'

Dressed in his familiar old blue suit, looking more than ever as if he made a practice of sleeping in it, dark grey shirt and crimson tie, Moreland, hatless, seemed an improbable survival from pre-war life. He was flushed and breathing rather hard. This gave the impression of poorish health. His face, his whole person, was thinner. The flush increased when he recognised Lovell, who must at once have recalled thoughts of Priscilla. Even after this redness had died down, a certain discoloration of the skin remained, increasing the suggestion that Moreland was not well. There was a moment of awkwardness, in spite of Lovell's immediate display of satisfaction that they should have met again. This was chiefly because Moreland seemed unwilling to commit himself by sitting at our table; an old habit of his, one of those characteristic postponements of action for which he was always laughing at himself, like his constitutional inability in all circumstances to decide from a menu what he wanted to eat.

'I shall be taken for a spy if I sit with you both,' he said. 'Somehow I never expected you'd really be wearing uniform, Nick, even though I knew you were in the army. I must tell you of rather a menacing thing that happened the other day. Norman Chandler appeared on my doorstep to hear the latest musical gossip. He's also become an officer, and we went off to get some lunch at Foppa's, where neither of us had been since the beginning of the war. The downstairs room was shut, because the window had been broken by a bomb, so we went upstairs, where the club used to be. There we found a couple of seedy-looking characters who said the restaurant was closed. We asked where Foppa was to be found. They said they didn't know. They weren't at all friendly. Positively disagreeable. Then I suddenly grasped they thought we were after Foppa for being an Italian—wanted to intern him or something. An army type and a member of the Special Branch. It was obvious as soon as one thought of it.'

'The Special Branch must have changed a lot if they now dress like you, Hugh.'

'Not more than army officers, if they now look like Norman.'

'Anyway, take a seat,' said Lovell. 'What are you going to drink? How's your war been going, Hugh? Not drearier than mine, I feel sure, if you'll excuse the self-pity.'

Moreland laughed, now more at ease after telling the story about Chandler and himself; Foppa's restaurant, even if closed, providing a kind of frame to unite the three of us.

'I seem to have neutralised the death-wish for the moment,' he said. 'Raids are a great help in that. I was also momentarily cheered just now by finding the man with the peg-leg and patch over one eye still going. He was behind the London Pavilion this evening, playing *Softly Awakes My Heart*. Rather an individual version. One of the worst features of the war is the dearth of itinerant musicians, indeed of vagrants generally. For example, I haven't seen the cantatrice on crutches for years. As I seem equally unfitted for warlike duties, I've thought of filling the gap and becoming a street musician myself. Unfortunately, I'm such a poor executant.'

'There's a former music critic in our Public Relations

branch,' said Lovell. 'He says the great thing for musicians now is the RAF band.'

'Doubt if they'd take me,' said Moreland, 'though the idea of massed orchestras of drum and fife soaring across the sky is attractive. Which is your PR man's paper?'

Lovell mentioned the name of the critic, who turned out to be an admirer of Moreland's work. The two of them began to discuss musical matters, of which Lovell possessed a smattering, anyway as far as personalities were concerned, from days of helping to write a column. No one could have guessed from Lovell's manner that inwardly he was in a state of great disturbance. On the contrary, it was Moreland who, after a preliminary burst of talkativeness, reverted to an earlier uneasiness of manner. Something was on his mind. He kept shifting about in his seat, looking towards the door of the restaurant, as if expecting an arrival that might not be exactly welcome. This apparent nervousness brought to mind the unaccustomed tone of his postcard. It looked as if something had happened, which he lacked the will to explain.

'Are you dining with us?' he suddenly asked Lovell.

There was no reason why that enquiry should not be made. The tone was perfectly friendly. All the same, a touch of abruptness added to this sense of apprehension.

'Chips is going to the Madrid—I didn't realise places like that still functioned.'

'Not many of them do,' said Lovell. 'In any case I'm never asked to them. I've no doubt it will be a very sober affair compared with the old days. The only thing to be said is that Max Pilgrim is doing a revival there of some of his old songs—*Tess of Le Touquet, Heather, Heather, she's under the weather*, all those.'

'Max is our lodger now,' said Moreland unexpectedly.

'He may be looking in here later after his act. He's been with ENSA entertaining the forces—by his own account enjoying a spot of entertainment himself—and has been released to do this brief season at the Madrid as a kind of rest.'

I was curious to know who was included when Moreland spoke of 'our' lodger. A question on this subject might be more tactfully put after Lovell's withdrawal. It sounded as if someone had taken Matilda's place. Lovell spoke a word or two about the party ahead of him. He seemed unwilling to leave us.

'I've never been to the Madrid as a client,' said Moreland. 'I once went there years ago, so to speak to the stage door, to collect Max after his act, because we were having supper together. I remember his talking about your friend Bijou Ardglass then. Wasn't she mistress of some Balkan royalty?'

'Theodoric,' said Lovell, 'but they can't have met for years. That Scandinavian princess he married keeps Theodoric very much in order. They were both lucky to get away when they did. He's always been very pro-British and would have been in a bad way had the Germans got him when they overran the country. There's a small contingent of his own people over here now. They were training in France when the war came, and crossed at the time of Dunkirk. I say, I hope there'll be something to drink tonight. The wine outlook becomes increasingly desperate since France went. One didn't expect to have to fight a war on an occasional half-pint of bitter, and lucky if you find that. Well, it's been nice seeing you both. I'll keep in touch, Nick, about those various points.'

We said goodbye to him. Lovell left for the Madrid. Moreland showed signs of relief that he was no longer with us. At first I thought this was still, as it were, on account of Priscilla; or, like some people—amongst whom several of his own relations were included—he simply found Lovell's company tedious. As it turned out, both possibilities were incorrect. Quite another matter was on Moreland's mind. This was only revealed when I suggested it was time to order dinner. Moreland hesitated.

'Do you mind if we wait a minute or two longer?' he said. 'Audrey thought she'd probably get away in time to join us for some food.'

'Audrey who?'

'Audrey Maclintick—you know her.'

He spoke sharply, as if the question had been a silly one to ask.

'Maclintick's wife—the one who went off with the violinist?'

'Yes—Maclintick's widow, rather. I always assume everyone is familiar with the rough outlines of my own life, such as they are. I suppose, as a gallant soldier, you live rather out of the world of rank and fashion. Audrey and I are running steady now.'

'Under the same roof?'

'In my old flat. I found I could get back there, owing to the blitz and it being left empty, so took the opportunity to move in again.'

'And Max Pilgrim is your lodger?'

'Has been for some months.'

Moreland had been embarrassed by having to explain so specifically that he was now living with Mrs Maclintick, but seemed glad this fact was made plain. There had been no avoiding a pointblank enquiry about the situation; nor was all surprise possible to conceal. He must certainly have been conscious that, to any friend not already aware

he and Mrs Maclintick had begun to see each other fre-
quently, the news must come as an incalculable reversal
of former circumstances and feelings.

'Life became rather impossible after Matilda left me,' he
said.

He spoke almost apologetically, at the same time seemed
to find relief in expressing how the present situation had
come about. The statement that life for him had become
'impossible' after Matilda's departure was easy to believe.
Without Matilda, the organisation of Moreland's day was
hard to imagine. Formerly she had arranged almost all the
routine of those affairs not immediately dictated by his
profession. In that respect, unless she had greatly changed,
Mrs Maclintick could hardly be proving an adequate
substitute. On the one or two occasions when, in the past,
I had myself encountered Mrs Maclintick, she had
appeared to me, without qualification, as one of the least
sympathetic of women. So far as that went, in those days
she had been in the habit of showing towards Moreland
himself sentiments not much short of active dislike. He
had been no better disposed to her, though, as an old
friend of Maclintick's, always doing his best to keep the
peace between them as husband and wife. When she had
left Maclintick for Carolo, Moreland's sympathies were
certainly on Maclintick's side. In short, this was another of
war's violent readjustments; possibly to be revealed under
close investigation as more logical than might appear at
first sight. Indeed, as Moreland began to expand the story,
as so often happens, the unthinkable took on the authorita-
tive tone of something that had to be.

'After Audrey bolted with Carolo, they kept together
till the beginning of the war—surprising in a way, knowing them both, it went on so long. Then he left her for a

girl in a repertory company. Audrey remained on her own. She was working in a canteen when we ran across each other—still is. She's coming on from there tonight.'

'I never heard a word about you and her.'

'We don't get on too badly,' said Moreland. 'I haven't been specially well lately. That bloody lung. Audrey's been very good about looking after me.'

He still seemed to feel further explanation, or excuse, was required; at the same time he was equally anxious not to appear dissatisfied with the new alignment.

'Maclintick doing himself in shook me up horribly,' he said. 'Of course, there can be no doubt Audrey was partly to blame for that, leaving him flat as she did. All the same, she was fond of Maclintick in her way. She often talks of him. You know you get to a stage, especially in wartime, when it's a relief to hear familiar things talked about, whatever they are, and whoever's saying them. You don't care what line the conversation takes apart from that. For instance, Maclintick's unreadable book on musical theory he was writing. It was never finished by him, much less published. His last night alive, as a final gesture against the world, Maclintick tore the manuscript into small pieces and stopped up the lavatory with it. That was just before he turned the gas on. You'd be surprised how much Audrey knows about what Maclintick said in that book— on the technical side, I mean, which she's no training in or taste for. In an odd way, I like knowing about all that. It's almost as if Maclintick's still about—though if he were, of course, I shouldn't be living with Audrey. Here she is, anyway.'

Mrs Maclintick was moving between the tables, making in our direction. She wore a three-quarter length coat over trousers, a rather notably inelegant form of female dress popular at that moment in circumstances where no formality was required. I remembered that Gypsy Jones—La Passionaria of Hendon Central, as Moreland himself had called her—had heralded in her own person the advent of this mode, when Widmerpool and I had seen her addressing a Communist anti-war meeting from a soapbox at a street corner. The clothes increased Mrs Maclintick's own air of being a gipsy, one in fact, rather than just in name. Moreland's nostalgia for vagrancy was recalled, too, by her appearance, which immediately suggested telling fortunes if her palm was crossed with silver, selling clothes-pegs, or engaging in any other traditional Romany activity. By way of contrast with this physical exterior, she entirely lacked any of the ingratiating manner commonly associated with the gipsy's role. Small, wiry, aggressive, she looked as ready as ever for a row, her bright black eyes and unsmiling countenance confronting a world from which perpetual hostility was not merely potential, but presumptive. Attack, she made clear, would be met with counter-attack. However, in spite of this embattled appearance, discouraging to anyone who had ever witnessed her having a row with Maclintick, she seemed disposed at this particular moment to make herself agreeable; more agreeable, at any rate, than on earlier occasions when we had run across each other.

'Moreland told me you would be here,' she said. 'We don't get out to this sort of place much nowadays—can't afford it—but when we do we're glad to meet friends.'

She spoke as if I had a trifle blatantly imposed myself on a party of their own, rather than herself converged on a meeting specially arranged between Moreland and myself. At the same time her tone was not antagonistic; indeed, by her pre-war standards, in as much as I knew them, it was positively amiable. It occurred to me she perhaps saw her association with Moreland as a kind of revenge on Maclintick, who had so greatly valued him as a friend. Now, Maclintick was underground and Moreland belonged to her. Moreland himself, whose earlier state of nerves had certainly been provoked by the prospect of having to present himself and Mrs Maclintick as a ménage, now looked relieved, the immediate impact manoeuvred without disaster. Characteristically, he began to embark on one of those dissertations about life in which he was habitually inclined to indulge after some awkwardness had arisen. It had been just the same when he used to feel with Matilda that the ice was thin for conversational skating and would deliberately switch from the particular to the general.

'Since war prevents any serious work,' he said, 'I have been trying to think out a few things. Make my lymphatic brain function a little. All part of my retreat from perfectionism. Besides, one really must hold one or two firm opinions on matters before one's forty—a doom about to descend before any of us know where we are. I find war clears the mind in a few respects. At least that can be said for it.'

I was reminded how Stringham, too, had remarked that he was thinking things out, though it was hard to decide whether 'perfectionism' played much part in Stringham's problems. Perhaps it did. That was one explanation. In Moreland's case, there could be no doubt Mrs Maclintick herself was an element in this retreat. In her case, indeed, so far as Moreland was concerned, withdrawal from perfectionism had been so unphased as to constitute an operation reasonably to be designated a rout. Perhaps Mrs Maclintick herself, even if the awareness remained undefined in her mind, felt she must be regarded as implicit in this advertised new approach—therefore some sort of protest should be made—because, although she spoke without savagery, her next words were undoubtedly a call to order.

'The war doesn't seem to clear your mind quite enough, Moreland,' she said. 'I only wish it stopped you dreaming a bit. Guess where that lost ration card of yours turned up, after I'd looked for it up hill and down dale. *In the toilet.* Bettter than nowhere, I suppose. Saved me from standing in a queue at the Town Hall for a couple of hours to get you another one—and when was I going to find time for that, I wonder.'

She might have been addressing a child. Since she herself had never given birth—had, I remembered, expressed active objection to being burdened with offspring—Moreland may to some extent have occupied a child's role in her eyes; possibly even in her needs, something she had sought in Maclintick and never found. Moreland, so far as it went, seemed to accept this status, receiving the complaint with a laugh, though no denial of its justice.

'I must have dropped it there before fire-watching,' he said. 'How bored one gets on those nights. It's almost worse, if there isn't a raid. I began to plan a work, last time, called *The Fire-watcher's March,* drums, you know, perhaps triangle and oboe. I was feeling particularly fed up that night, not just displeased with the war, or certain social or political conditions from which one suffers, but tired of the whole thing. That is one of the conceptions most difficult for stupid people to grasp. They always suppose some ponderable alteration will make the human condition more bearable. The only hope of survival is the realisation that no such thing could possibly happen.'

'Never mind what goes through your head when you're

fire-watching, Moreland,' said Mrs Maclintick. 'You order some dinner. We don't want to starve to death while you hold forth. It won't be much when it comes, if I'm any prophet.'

These words were another reminder of going out with Moreland and Matilda, though Matilda's remonstrance would have been less downright. The plea for food was reasonable enough. We got hold of a waiter. There was the usual business of Moreland being unable to decide, even from the limited choice available, what he wanted to eat. In due course dinner arrived. Moreland, now back on his accustomed form, discoursed about his work and people we knew. Mrs Maclintick, grumbling about domestic difficulties, showed herself in general amenable. The evening was turning out a success. One change, however, was to be noticed in Moreland's talk. When he dwelt on the immediate past, it was as if all that had become very distant, no longer the matter of a year or two before. For him, it was clear, a veil, a thick curtain, had fallen between 'now' and 'before the war'. He would suddenly become quite worked up about people we had known, parties we had been to, subjects for amusement we had experienced together, laughing at moments so violently that tears ran down his cheeks. One felt he was fairly near to other, deeper emotions, that the strength of his feelings was due to something in addition to a taste for mulling over moments in retrospect enjoyable or grotesque.

'You must admit funny things did happen in the old days,' he said. 'Maclintick's story about Dr Trelawney and the red-haired succubus that could only talk Hebrew.'

'Oh, don't go on about the old days so,' said Mrs Macklintick. 'You make me feel a hundred. Try and live in the present for a change. For instance, it might interest you to know that a one-time girl friend of yours is about to sit down at a table over there.'

We looked in the direction she had indicated by jerking her head. It was perfectly true. Priscilla Lovell and an officer in battle-dress were being shown to a table not far from our own. The officer was Odo Stevens. For a moment they were occupied with a waiter, so that a brief suspension of time was offered to consider how best to deal with this encounter, superlatively embarrassing, certainly soon unavoidable. At first it struck me as a piece of quite undeserved, almost incredible ill chance that they should turn up like this; but, on consideration, especially in the light of what Lovell himself had told me, there was nothing specially odd about it. Probably Stevens was on leave. This was an obvious enough place to dine, though certainly not one to choose if you wanted to be discreet.

'Adulterers are always asking the courts for discretion,' Peter Templer used to say, 'when, as a rule, discretion is the last thing they've been generous with themselves.'

If Priscilla thought her husband still stationed on the East Coast, she would of course not expect to meet him here. On the face of it, there was no reason why she should not dine with Stevens, if he happened to be passing through London. A second's thought showed that what seemed a piece of preposterous exhibitionism only presented that appearance on account of special knowledge acquired from Lovell. All the same, if Priscilla were dining here, that meant she had cut the Bijou Ardglass party. So unpredictably do human beings behave, she might even plan to take Stevens on there later.

'Is that her husband with her?' asked Mrs Maclintick. 'I've never had the pleasure of meeting him. I suppose you look on him as the man who cut you out, Moreland?'

I was surprised she knew about Moreland's former entanglement with Priscilla. No doubt Maclintick had spoken of it in the past. As Moreland himself had remarked, she and Maclintick must, at least some of the time, have enjoyed a closer, more amicable existence together than their acquaintances inclined to suppose. The Maclinticks could even have met Moreland and Priscilla at some musical event. Anyway, Mrs Maclintick had turned out to know Priscilla by sight, had evidently gathered scraps of her story, at least so far as Moreland was concerned. That was all. She could not also be aware of other implications disturbing to myself. So far as Mrs Maclintick's knowledge went, therefore, Priscilla's presence might be regarded as merely personally displeasing, in her capacity as a former love of Moreland's. However, so developed was Mrs Maclintick's taste for malice, like everyone of her kind, that she seemed to know instinctively something inimical to myself, too, was in the air. Moreland, on the other hand, having talked with Lovell only a short time before, could not fail to suspect trouble of one sort or another was on foot. Never very good at concealing his feelings, he went red again. This change of colour was no doubt chiefly caused by Mrs Maclintick's not too delicate reference to himself, but probably he guessed something of my own sentiments as well.

'The girl's Nick's sister-in-law,' he said. 'You seem to have forgotten that. I don't know who the army type is.'

'Oh, yes, she's your sister-in-law, isn't she,' said Mrs Macklintick. 'Now I remember. Not bad looking. Got herself up for the occasion too, hasn't she?'

Mrs Maclintick did not elaborate why she thought Priscilla's clothes deserved this comment, though they were certainly less informal than her own outfit. Priscilla's appearance, at its most striking, made her not far short of a 'beauty'. She looked striking enough now, though not in the best of humours. Her fair hair was longer than at Frederica's, her face thinner. There was about her that taut, at the same time supple air, the yielding movement of body women sometimes display when conducting a love affair, like the physical pose of an athlete observed between contests. She had a high colour. Stevens, apparently in the best of spirits, was talking noisily. No escape was offered, even though they were the last people I wanted to run into at that moment. It seemed wise to prepare the ground with some explanation of why these two might reasonably be out together. This was perhaps instinctive, rather than logical, because Lovell himself had spoken as if the whole world knew about the affair.

'The man's called Odo Stevens. I was on a course with him.'

'Oh, you know him, do you?' said Mrs Maclintick. 'He looks a bit . . .'

She did not finish the sentence. Although her comment was never revealed, one had the impression she grasped pretty well the essential aspects of Odo Stevens, even if only the superficial ones. No great psychological powers were required to make a reasonably accurate guess at these, anyway for immediate practical purposes, whatever might be found deeper down. At that moment Stevens caught sight of us. He waved. Then, at once, he spoke to Priscilla, who herself looked in our direction. She too waved, at the same time began to say something to Stevens. Whatever that was, he disregarded it. Jumping up, he came towards our table. The only hope now was that Mrs Maclintick's uncompromising manner might save the situation by causing Stevens to feel himself unwelcome; if not drive him off entirely, at least discourage a long conversation. She could easily make matters more bizarre than embarrassing. I felt suddenly grateful for her presence. However, as things fell out, Mrs Maclintick was not placed in the position of exercising an active role. This was on account of Stevens himself. I had completely underestimated the change that had taken place in him. Never lacking in self-confidence, at Aldershot he had at the same time been undecided how best to present himself; how, so to speak, to get the maximum value from his own personality. He held various cards in his hand—as I had tried to explain to Lovell—most of them good ones. At different times he would vary the line he took: rough diamond: ambitious young provincial salesman: journalist on the make: soldier of fortune: professional womaniser. Those were just a few of them, all played with a reasonable lightness of touch. Stevens was certainly aware, too, of possibility to charm by sheer lack of any too exact a definition of personality or background. Some of this vagueness of outline may have had a fascination for Priscilla. Now, however, he had enormously added to the effectiveness of his own social attack, immediately giving the impression, as he approached our table, that he was prepared to take on this, or any other party of people, off his own bat. He himself was going to do the entertaining. No particular co-operation from anyone else was required. He had put up an additional pip since we last met, but, although still only a lieutenant, he wore the mauve and white ribbon of an MC, something of a rarity in acquisition at this comparatively early stage of the war.

'Well, old cock,' he said. 'Fancy meeting you here. This is a bit of luck. What are you up to? On leave, or stationed in London?'

Before I could answer, Priscilla herself came up to the table. She had followed Stevens almost at once. There was not much else for her to do. Even if she might have preferred to postpone a meeting, in due course inevitable, or, like myself, hoped to reduce contacts to no more than a nod or brief word at the end of the evening, Stevens had given her no chance to impede his own renewal of acquaintance. His principle was to work on impulse. Nothing could have prevented him from making the move he had. Now that had taken place, she no doubt judged the best tactical course was to ally herself with this explosive greeting; as good a way of handling the situation as any other, if it had to be handled at all. Besides, Priscilla may have felt that, by joining us, she could keep an eye on Stevens; modify, if necessary, whatever he might say.

'Yes, why are you here, Nick?' she asked, speaking challengingly, as if I, rather than her, found myself in doubtful company. 'I thought you were miles away across the sea. And Hugh—how marvellous to see you again after so long. I was listening to something of yours in a BBC programme last week.'

She was perfectly self-possessed. If aware of rumours afloat about herself and Stevens—of which she could hardly be ignorant, had she bothered to give a moment's thought to the matter—Priscilla was perfectly prepared to brazen these out. The two of them could not know, of course, how narrowly they had missed Lovell himself. Perhaps, again, neither cared. Lovell's taste for drama would certainly have been glutted, had they arrived an hour or so earlier. In the group we now formed, Moreland was the one who seemed most embarrassed. Conventionally speaking, he had not risen to the occasion very successfully. His highly developed intuitive faculties had instantly registered something was amiss; while the mere fact he had himself once been in love with Priscilla was, in any case, enough to agitate him, when unexpectedly confronted with her. No doubt he was also piqued at her coming on him in circumstances which must reveal sooner or later he and Mrs Maclintick were making a life together. He muttered something or other about whatever composition Priscilla had heard on the radio, but seemed unable to pursue any coherent conversation. Mrs Maclintick stared at Stevens without friendliness, though a good deal of curiosity, a reception that seemed perfectly to satisfy him.

'Look here,' he said. 'Are you all having a very special private party? If not, couldn't we come and sit with you? This is the chance of a lifetime to make a jolly evening of my last night in London for a long time—who knows, perhaps for ever. I'm on embarkation leave, you know, have to catch a train back to my unit tonight.'

He began addressing this speech to me, but, halfway through, turned towards Mrs Maclintick, as if to appeal to her good nature. She did not offer much encouragement; at the same time issued no immediate refusal.

'Anything you like,' she said. 'I'm too tired to care much what happens. Been on my feet all day doling out shepherd's pie made of sausage meat and stale swiss roll all minced up together. But don't expect Moreland to pay. I've let him have enough out of the house-keeping money to cover our share of dinner—and an extra round of drinks if we can get that.'

Moreland made some sort of protest at this, half amused, half ashamed. Stevens, obviously assessing Mrs Maclintick's measure at a glance (just as Stringham had, at the party years before after Moreland's symphony), laughed loudly. She glared at him for treating her self-pity so lightly, but, although fierce in expression, her stare was not entirely one of dislike.

'We'll be absolutely self-supporting, I promise that,' said Stevens. 'I've only got a quid or two left myself, but Priscilla cashed a cheque earlier in the day, so we'll have to prise it out of her if necessary.'

'You may not find that so easy,' said Priscilla, laughing too, though perhaps not best pleased at this indication of being permanently in the company of Stevens. 'In the end Nick will probably have to fork out, as a relation. Will it really be all right if we join you, Nick?'

Although she said this lightly, in the same sort of vein used by Stevens himself, she spoke now with less assurance than he. Certainly she would, in any case, have preferred no such suggestion to be made. Once put, she was not going to run counter to it. She was determined to support her lover, show nothing was going to intimidate her. No doubt she had hoped to spend the evening tête-à-tête with him, especially if this were his last night in England. Even apart from that, there was, from her own point of view, nothing whatever to be said for deliberately joining a group of people that included a brother-in-law. On the other hand, she had perhaps already learnt the impossibility of dissuading Stevens from doing things the way he wanted them done. Perhaps, again, that was one of the attractions he exercised, in contrast with Lovell, usually amenable in most social matters. Stevens clearly possessed one of those personalities that require constant reinforcement for their egotism and energy by the presence and attention of other people round them, an audience to whom they can 'show off'. Such men are attractive to women, at the same time hard for women to keep at heel. For my own part, I would much rather have prevented the two of them from sitting with us, but, short of causing what might almost amount to a 'scene', there seemed no way of avoiding this. Even assuming I made some more or less discouraging gesture, that was likely to prove not only rather absurd, but also useless from Lovell's point of view; perhaps even undesirable where Lovell's interests were in question.

'I mean you look a bit uncertain, Nick?' said Priscilla, laughing again.

Obviously the thoughts going through my head were as clear as day to her.

'Don't be silly.'

'Half a minute,' said Stevens, 'I'll try and find a waiter and get another chair. We can't all cram together on the banquette.'

He went off. Mrs Maclintick began some complicated financial computation with Moreland. This was going to hold the attention of the pair of them for a minute or two. Priscilla had sat down, and, perhaps because she felt herself more vulnerable without Stevens, had her head down, fumbling in her bag, as if she wanted to avoid my eye. I felt some statement should be made which might, at least to some small extent, define my own position. It was now or never. Any such 'statement' was, I thought, to be conceived of as the term is made use of by the police, for the description of an accident or crime, a brief summary of what happened, how and why it took place or was committed.

'I had a drink with Chips this evening.'

She looked up.

'*Chips?*'

'Here—just before dinner. He thought he might see you at Bijou Ardglass' party at the Madrid.'

That information would at least prevent her from taking Stevens to the restaurant, had the thought been in her mind, though, at the same time, could prejudice any faint chance of herself looking in at the Ardglass party after Stevens had left to catch his train. Such a possibility had to be faced. A chance must be taken on that. It was, in any case, unlikely she would go later to the Madrid. Everything would close down by midnight at the latest, probably before that.

'Oh, but is Chips in London?'

She was plainly surprised.

'At Combined Ops.'

'On the Combined Ops staff?'

'Yes.'

'That was only a possibility when I last heard.'

'It's happened.'

'Chips thought the move wouldn't be for a week or two, even if it came off. His last letter only reached me this morning. It chased all over the country after me. I'm at Aunt Molly's.'

'I'll give you the Combined Ops number and extension.'

'I had to put Bijou off,' she said quite calmly. 'I'll get in touch with Chips tomorrow.'

'He thought you might be at the Jeavonses'.'

'Why didn't he ring up then?'

'He hoped he was going to see you at the Madrid—make a surprise of it.'

She did not rise to that.

'The Jeavons house is more of a shambles than ever,' she said. 'Eleanor Walpole-Wilson is there—Aunt Molly usen't to like her, but they're great buddies now—and then there are two Polish officers whose place was bombed and had nowhere to go, and a girl who's having a baby by a Norwegian sailor.'

'Who's having a baby by a Norwegian sailor?' asked Stevens. 'No one we know, I hope.'

He had come back to the table at that moment. Such as it was, my demonstration had been made, was now, of necessity, over. There was nothing more to be said. The situation could only be accepted, until, in one field or another, further action might be required. That, at least, was so far as I myself was concerned. Recognition of this as a fact seemed unavoidable. The return of Stevens brought about a reshuffle of places, resulting in Mrs Maclintick finding herself next him on the banquette with me on the other side of her. Priscilla and Moreland were opposite. This seating had been chiefly organised by Stevens himself, possibly with no more aim than a display of power. I congratulated him on his MC.

'Oh, that?' he said. 'Pretty hot stuff to have one of those, isn't it? I really deserved it—we both did—for putting up with that Aldershot course where we first met. It was far more gruelling than anything expected of me later—those lectures on the German army. Christ, I dream about them. Are you at the War House or somewhere?'

'On leave—going down to the country tomorrow.'

'Hope you have as much fun on it as I've had on mine,' he said.

He seemed totally unaware that, among members of Priscilla's family—myself, for example—conventional reservations might exist regarding the part he was at that moment playing; that at least they might not wish to hear rubbed in what an enjoyable time he had been having as her lover. All the same, shamelessness of any kind, perhaps rightly, always exacts a certain respect. Lovell himself was no poor hand at displaying cheek. As usual, a kind of poetic justice was observable in what was happening.

'I suppose your destination is secret?'

'Don't quote me, but there's been a tropical issue.'

'Middle East?'

'That's my opinion.'

'Might be the Far East.'

'You never know. I think the other myself.'

Until then Moreland had been sitting in silence, apparently unable, or unwilling, to cope with the changed composition of the party at the table. This awkwardness with new arrivals had always been a trait of his, and probably had little or nothing to do with the comparatively unfamiliar note struck by the personality and conversation of Stevens. A couple of middle-aged music critics he had known all his life might have brought about just the same sort of temporary stoppage in Moreland's conversation. Later, he would recover; talk them off their feet. Now, this change took place, he spoke with sudden animation.

'My God, I wish I could be transplanted to the Far East without further delay,' he said. 'I'd be prepared to be like Brahms and play the piano in a brothel—even play Brahms's own compositions in a brothel, part of the *Requiem* would be very suitable—if I could only be somewhere like Saigon or Bangkok, leave London and the blackout behind.'

'A naval officer I talked to on a bus the other day, just back from Hong-Kong, reported life there as bloody amusing,' said Stevens. 'But look, Mr Moreland, there's something I must tell you before we go any further. Of course, I wanted to see Nicholas again, that was why I came over, but another pretty considerable item was that I had recognised you. I saw a chance of telling you personally what a fan of yours I am. Hearing your *Tone Poem Vieux Port* performed at Birmingham was one of the high spots of my early life. I was about sixteen, I suppose. You've probably forgotten Birmingham ever had a chance of hearing it, or you yourself ever came there. I haven't. I've always wanted to meet you and say how much it thrilled me.'

This was an unexpected trump card for Stevens to play. Moreland, always modest about his own works, showed permissible signs of pleasure at this sudden hearty praise from such an unexpected source. Music was an entirely new line from Stevens, so far as I knew him, until this moment. Obviously it constituted a weapon in his armoury, perhaps a formidable one. He had certainly opened up operations on an extended front since our weeks together at Aldershot. Mrs Maclintick broke in at this point.

'*Vieux Port*'s the one Maclintick always liked,' she said. 'He used to go on about that piece of music until I told him never to mention the thing to me again.'

'When it was performed at Birmingham, Maclintick was about the only critic who offered any praise,' said Moreland. 'Even that old puss Gossage was barely civil. The rest of the critics buried my music completely and me with it. I feel now like Nero meeting in Hades the unknown mourner who strewed flowers on his grave.'

'You're not in your grave yet, Moreland,' said Mrs Maclintick, 'nor even in Hades, though you always talk as if you were. I never knew such a morbid man.'

'I meant the grave of my works rather than my own,' said Moreland. 'That's what it looked like that year at Birmingham. Anyway, not being dead's no argument against feeling like Nero. Quite the reverse.'

'Not much hope of a Roman orgy here,' said Stevens. 'Even the food's hard to wallow in, don't you agree, Mrs Maclintick?'

He turned his attention to her, in the manner of his particular brand of narcissism, determined to make a conquest, separate and individual, of everyone sitting at the table.

'From the way you talk,' he said, 'you don't sound as great a Moreland fan as you should be. Fancy saying you got tired of hearing *Vieux Port* praised. I'm surprised at you.'

'I'm a fan all right,' said Mrs Maclintick. 'Not half, I am. You should see him in bed in the morning before he's shaved. You couldn't help being a fan then.'

There was some laughter at that, in which Moreland himself joined loudly, though he would probably have preferred his relationship with Mrs Maclintick to have been expressed less explicitly in the presence of Priscilla. At the same time, Mrs Maclintick's tone had been not without affection of a kind. The reply she had made, whether or not with that intention, hindered Stevens from continuing to discuss Moreland's music more or less seriously, an object he seemed to have in view. However, this did not prevent him from increasing, if only in a routine manner, his own air of finding Mrs Maclintick attractive, a policy that was beginning to make a good impression on her. This behaviour, however light-hearted, was perhaps displeasing to Priscilla, no doubt unwilling to admit to herself that, for Stevens, one woman was, at least up to a point, as good as another; anyway when sitting in a restaurant. She may reasonably have felt that no competition should be required of her to keep him to herself. There was, of course, no question of Stevens showing any real interest in Mrs Maclintick, but, in circumstances prevailing, Priscilla probably regarded all his attention as belonging to herself alone. Whether or not this was the reason, she had become quite silent. Now she interrupted the conversation.

'Listen . . .'

'What?'

'I believe there's a blitz on.'

We all stopped talking for a moment. A faint suggestion of distant gunfire merged into the noise of traffic from the street, the revving up of a lorry's engine somewhere just outside the back of the building. No one else at the other tables round about showed any sign of noticing indications of a raid.

'I don't think so,' said Moreland. 'Living in London all the time, one gets rather a good ear for the real thing.'

'Raids when I'm on leave make me bloody jumpy,' said Stevens. 'Going into action you've got a whole lot of minor responsibilities to keep your mind off the danger. A gun, too. In an air-raid I feel they're after me, and there's nothing I can do about it.'

I asked how much hand-to-hand fighting he had been engaged in.

'The merest trifle.'

'What was it like?'

'Not too bad.'

'Hard on the nerves?'

'Difficult to describe,' he said. 'You feel worked up just before, of course, rather like going to school for the first time or the morning of your first job. Those prickly sensations, but exciting too.'

'Going back to school?' said Moreland. 'You make warfare sound most disturbing. I shouldn't like that at all.

In London, it's the sheer lack of sleep gets one down. However, there's been quite a let-up the last day or two. Do you have raids where you are, Nick?'

'We do.'

'I thought it was all very peaceful there.'

'Not always.'

'I have an impression of acute embarrassment when bombed,' said Moreland. 'That rather than gross physical fear—at present anyway. It's like an appalling display of bad manners one has been forced to witness. The utter failure of a party you are giving—a friend's total insensitiveness about some delicate matter—suddenly realising you've lost your note-case, your passport, your job, your girl. All those things combined and greatly multiplied.'

'You didn't like it the other night when the glass shattered in the bathroom window,' said Mrs Maclintick. 'You were trembling like a leaf, Moreland.'

'I don't pretend to be specially brave,' said Moreland, put out by this comment. 'Anyway, I'd just run up three flights of stairs and nearly caught it in the face. I was merely trying to define the sensation one feels—don't you agree, Nick, it's a kind of embarrassment?'

'Absolutely.'

'Depends on such a lot of different things,' said Stevens. 'People you're with, sleep, food, drink, and so on. This show I was in——'

He did not finish the sentence, because Priscilla interrupted. She had gone rather white. For a second one saw what she would be like when she was old.

'For God's sake don't talk about the war all the time,' she said. 'Can't we sometimes get away from it for a few seconds?'

This was quite different from her earlier detached tone.

138

She seemed all at once in complete despair. Stevens, not best pleased at having his story wrecked, mistook the reason, whatever it was, for Priscilla's sudden agitation. He thought she was afraid, altogether a misjudgment.

'But it isn't a blitz, sweetie,' he said. 'There's nothing to get worked up about.'

Although, in the light of his usual manner of addressing people, he might easily have called Mrs Maclintick 'sweetie', this was, in fact, the first time he had spoken to Priscilla with that mixture of sharpness and affection that can suddenly reveal an intimate relationship.

'I know it isn't a blitz,' she said. 'We long ago decided that. I was just finding the conversation boring.'

'All right. Let's talk of something else,' he said.

He spoke indulgently, but without grasping that something had gone badly wrong.

'I've got rather a headache.'

'Oh, sorry, darling. I thought you had the wind up.'

'Not in the least.'

'Why didn't you say you had a head?'

'It's only just started.'

She was looking furious now, furious and upset. I knew her well enough to be fairly used to Priscilla's quickly changing moods, but her behaviour was now inexplicable to me, as it obviously was to Stevens. I imagined that, having decided a mistake had been made in allowing him to join our table, she had now settled on a display of bad temper as the best means of getting him away.

'Well, what would you like to do?' he said. 'We've got nearly an hour still. Shall I take you somewhere quieter? It is rather airless and noisy in here.'

He seemed anxious to do anything he could to please her. Up till now they might have been any couple having dinner together, no suggestion of a particularly close bond, Stevens's ease of manner concealing rather than emphasising what was happening. Now, however, his voice showed a mixture of concern and annoyance that gave more away about the pair of them. This change of tone was certainly due to incomprehension on his part, rather than any exhibitionistic desire to advertise that Priscilla was his mistress; although he might well have been capable of proclaiming that fact in other company.

'Where?' she said.

This was not a question. It was a statement to express the truth that no place existed in this neighbourhood where they could go, and be likely to find peace and quiet.

'We'll look for somewhere.'

She fixed her eyes on him. There was silence for a moment.

'I think I'll make for home.'

'But aren't you coming to see me off—you said you were.'

'I've got a splitting headache,' she said. 'I've suddenly begun to feel perfectly awful, too, for some reason. Simply dreadful.'

'Not up to coming to the station?'

'Sorry.'

She was nearly in tears. Stevens plainly had no idea what had gone wrong. I could not guess either, unless the comparative indifference of his mood—after what had no doubt been a passionate interlude of several days—had upset her. Although young, and, until recently, probably not much accustomed to girls of Priscilla's type, he was sufficiently experienced with women in general to have certain settled principles in dealing with situations of this kind. At any rate, he was now quite decisive.

'I'll take you back then.'

Faced with the prospect of abandoning a party where he had begun to be enjoyably the centre of attention, Stevens spoke without a great deal of enthusiasm, at the same time with complete sincerity. The offer was a genuine one, not a polite fiction to be brushed aside on the grounds he had a train to catch. He intended to go through with the proposal. Certainly it was the least he could do, but, at the same time, considering Priscilla's demeanour and what I knew of his own character, even this minimum was to display magnanimity of a sort. He accepted her sudden decision with scarcely any demur. Priscilla seemed to appreciate that.

'No.'

She spoke quite firmly.

'Of course I will.'

'You've got all your stuff here. You can't lug it back to Kensington.'

'I'll pick it up here again after I've dropped you.'

'You can't do that.'

'Of course I can.'

'No . . .' she said. 'I'd much rather you didn't . . . I don't quite know . . . I just feel suddenly rather odd . . . I can't think what it is . . . I mean I'd rather be alone . . . Must be alone . . .'

The situation had become definitely very painful. Even Mrs Maclintick was silenced, awed by this interchange. Moreland kept on lighting cigarettes and stubbing them out. It all seemed to take hours of time.

'I'm going to take you back.'

'No, really no.'

'But——'

'I can take you back, Priscilla,' I said. 'Nothing easier.'

That settled things finally.

'I don't want anybody to take me back,' she said. 'I'll say goodbye now.'

She waved her hand in the direction of Stevens.

'I'll write,' she said.

He muttered something about getting a taxi for her, began to try and move out from where he was sitting. People leaving or arriving at the next table penned him in. Priscilla turned and made quickly for the glass doors. Just before she went through them, she turned and blew a kiss. Then she disappeared from sight. By the time Stevens had extracted himself, she was gone. All the same, he set off across the room to follow her.

'What a to-do all of a sudden,' said Mrs Maclintick. 'Did she behave like this when you knew her, Moreland?'

I thought it possible, though not very likely, that Priscilla had gone to look for Lovell at the Madrid. That surmise belonged to a way of life more dramatic than probable, the sort of development that would have greatly appealed to Lovell himself; in principle, I mean, even had he been in no way personally concerned. However, for better or worse, things like that do not often happen. At the same time, even though sudden desire to make it up with her husband might run contrary to expectation, I was no nearer conjecturing why Priscilla had gone off in this manner, leaving Stevens cold. The fact she might be in love with him was no reason to prevent a sudden display of capricious temper, brought on, likely as not, by the many stresses of the situation. Stevens himself was no doubt cynical enough in the way he was taking the affair, although even that was uncertain, since Lovell had supposed marriage could be in question. Lovell might be right. Stevens's false step, so far as Priscilla was concerned, seemed to be marked by the moment he had suggested her fear about the supposititous air-raid warning. That had certainly made her angry. Even allowing for unexpected nervous reactions in wartime, it was much more likely she heard an air-raid warning—where none existed—because of her highly strung state, rather than from physical fear. Stevens had shown less than his usual grasp in suggesting such a thing. Possibly this nervous state stemmed from some minor row; possibly Priscilla's poorish form earlier in the evening suggested that she was beginning to tire of Stevens, or feared he might be tiring of her. On the other hand, the headache, the thought of her lover's departure, could equally have upset her; while the presence of the rest of the party at the table, the news that her husband was in London, all helped to discompose her. Reasons for her behaviour were as hard to estimate as that for giving herself to Stevens in the first instance. If she merely wanted amusement, while Lovell's physical presence was removed by forces over which he had no control, why make all this trouble about it, why not keep things quiet? Lovell, at worst, appeared a husband preferable to many. Even if less indefatigably lively than Stevens, he was not without his own brand of energy. Was 'trouble', in fact, what Priscilla required? Was her need—the need of certain women—to make men unhappy? There was something of the kind in her face. Perhaps she was simply tormenting Stevens now for a change; so to speak, varying the treatment. If so, she might have her work cut out to disturb him in the way she was disturbing Lovell; had formerly disturbed Moreland. The fact that he was able to look after himself pretty well in that particular sphere was implicit in the manner Stevens made his way back across the room. He looked politely worried, not at all shattered.

'Did she get a taxi?'

'She must have done. She'd disappeared into the black-out by the time I got to the door on the street. There were several cabs driving away at that moment.'

'She did take on,' said Mrs Maclintick.

'It's an awful business,' said Stevens. 'The point is I'm so immobile myself at this moment. There's a lot of junk in the cloakroom here, a valise, God knows what else—odds and ends they wanted me to get for the Mess—all of which I've got to hump to the station before long.'

He looked at his watch; then sat down again at the table.

'Let's have some more to drink,' he said, 'that's if we can get it.'

For a short time he continued to show some appearance of being worried about Priscilla, expressing anxiety, asserting she had seemed perfectly all right earlier that evening. He reproached himself for not being able to do more to help her get home, wanting our agreement that there was anyway little or nothing he could have done. After repeating these things several times, he showed himself finally prepared to accept the fact that what had happened was all in the day's work where women were concerned.

'I'll ring up when I get to the station,' he said.

Priscilla's behaviour had positively stimulated Mrs Maclintick, greatly cheered her up.

'Whatever's wrong with the girl?' she said. 'Why does she want to go off like that? I believe she didn't approve of me wearing these filthy old clothes. Got to, doing the job I do. No good dressing up as if you were going to a wedding. You know her, Moreland. What was it all about?'

'I haven't the least idea,' said Moreland sharply.

He showed no wish to discuss Priscilla's conduct further. If, once or twice that evening, he had already brought a reminder of his behaviour when out with Matilda, now, by the tone he used, he recalled Maclintick out with Mrs Maclintick. She may have recognised that herself, because she pursed her lips.

'Wonder what's happened to Max,' she said. 'He should have been along by now. That turn must be over. It's a short one anyway, and he comes on early at the Madrid.'

'Probably gone to bed,' said Moreland.

Mrs Maclintick agreed that must have happened.

'More sense than sitting about in a place like this,' she added, 'especially if you've got to get up early in the morning like I have.'

'That's not Max Pilgrim you're talking about?' asked Stevens.

'He's our lodger,' said Moreland.

Stevens showed interest. Moreland explained he had known Pilgrim for years.

'I've always hoped to see him do his stuff,' said Stevens. 'There was a chance at this revival of his old songs at the Madrid—I suppose that's what he was coming on here from. I read about it in the paper and wanted to go, but Priscilla wouldn't hear of it. I can see now she hasn't been herself all day. I ought to have guessed she might be boiling up for a scene. You should know how girls are going to behave after you've been with them for a bit. I see I was largely to blame. She said she'd seen Pilgrim before and he bored her to hell. I told her I thought his songs marvellous. In fact I used to try and write stuff like that myself.'

I asked if he had ever sold anything of that sort to magazines.

'Only produced it for private consumption,' he said,

laughing. 'The sole verses I ever placed was sentimental stuff in the local press. They wouldn't have liked my Max Pilgrim line, if it could be called that.'

'Let's hear some of it,' said Moreland.

He had evidently taken a fancy to Stevens, who possessed in his dealings that energetic, uninhibited impact which makes its possessor master of the immediate social situation; though this mastery always requires strong consolidating forces to keep up the initial success. Mr Deacon used to say nothing spread more ultimate gloom at a party than an exuberant manner which has roused false hopes. Stevens did not do that. He could summon more than adequate powers of consolidation after his preliminary attack. The good impression he had made on Moreland was no doubt helped, as things stood, by Priscilla's departure. Moreland wanted to forget about her, start off on a new subject. Stevens was just the man for that. Mention of his verse offered the channel. There were immediate indications that Stevens would not need much pressing about giving an example of his own compositions.

'For instance, I wrote something about my first unit when I was with them,' he said.

'Recite it to us.'

Stevens laughed, a merely formal gesture of modesty. He turned to me.

'Nicholas,' he said, 'were you ever junior subaltern in your battalion?'

'For what seemed a lifetime.'

'And proposed the King's health in the Mess on guest nights?'

'Certainly.'

'*Mr Vice, the Loyal Toast*—then you rose to your feet and said: *Gentlemen, the King*.'

146

'Followed by *The Allied Regiments*—such-and-such a regiment of Canada and such-and-such a regiment of Australia.'

'Do you mean to say this actually happened to you yourself, Nick?' asked Moreland. 'You stood up and said *Gentlemen, the King*?'

He showed total incredulity.

'I used to love it,' said Stevens. 'Put everything I had into the words. It was the only thing I liked about the dump. I only asked all this because I wrote some lines called *Guest Night*.'

'Shoot them off,' said Moreland.

Stevens cleared his throat, then, without the least self-consciousness, began his recitation in a low, dramatic voice:

> 'On Thursday it's a parade to dine,
>   The Allied Regiments and the King
> Are pledged in dregs of tawny wine,
>   But now the Colonel's taken wing.
>
> Yet subalterns still talk and tease
>   (Wide float the clouds of Craven A
> Stubbed out in orange peel and cheese)
>   Of girls and Other Ranks and pay.
>
> If—on last night-scheme—B Coy broke
>   The bipod of the borrowed bren:
> The Sergeants' Mess is out of coke:
>   And Gordon nearly made that Wren.
>
> Along the tables of the Mess
>   The artificial tulips blow,
> Tired as a prostitute's caress
>   Their crimson casts no gladdening glow.

Why do those phallic petals fret
The heart, till coils—like Dannert wire—
Concentrically expand regret
For lost true love and found desire?

While Haw-Haw, from the radio,
Aggrieved, insistent, down the stair,
With distant bugles, sweet and low,
Commingles on the winter air.'

Stevens ceased to declaim. He smiled and sat back in his seat. He was certainly unaware of the entirely new conception of himself his own spoken verses had opened up for me. Their melancholy revealed quite another side of his nature, one concealed as a rule by aggressive cheerfulness. This melancholy was no doubt a logical counterpart, the reverse surface of the coin, one to be expected from high spirits of his own particular sort, bound up as they were with a perpetual discharge of personality. All the same, one never learns to expect the obvious. This contrast of feeling in him might have been an element that attracted Priscilla, something she recognised when they first met at Frederica's; something more fundamentally melodramatic, even, than Lovell himself could achieve. We all expressed appreciation. Moreland was, I think, almost as surprised as myself.

'Not much like Max's stuff though,' he said.

'All the same, Max Pilgrim was the source.'

'Nor very cheerful,' said Mrs Maclintick. 'I do believe you're as morbid as Moreland is himself.'

Although she spoke in her accustomed spirit of depreciation, Stevens must have achieved his aim in making more or less of a conquest, because she smiled quite kindly at him after saying that. Moved by her complaisance, or, more likely, by the repetition of his own lines, his face registered self-pity.

'I wasn't feeling very cheerful at the time,' he said. 'That unit I went to as a one-pipper fairly got me down.'

Then, immediately, one of those instantaneous changes of mood, that were so much a part of him, took place.

'Would you like to hear one of the bawdy ones?' he asked.

Before anyone could reply, another officer, a big captain with a red face and cropped hair, like Stevens also wearing battle-dress, passed our table. Catching sight of Stevens, this man began to roar with laughter and point.

'Odo, my son,' he yelled. 'Fancy seeing your ugly mug here.'

'God, Brian, you old swine.'

'I suppose you've been painting the town red, and, like me, have got to catch the night train back to the bloody grind again. I've been having a pretty wet weekend, I can tell you.'

'Come and have a drink, Brian. There's lots of time.'

'Not going to risk being cashiered for WOASAWL.'

'What on earth's that he said?' asked Mrs Maclintick.

'While-On-Active-Service-Absent-Without-Leave,' said Stevens, characteristically not allowing her even for a second out of his power by disregarding the question. 'Oh, come on, Brian, no hurry yet.'

The red-faced captain was firm.

'Got to find a taxi, for one thing. Besides, I've baggage to pick up.'

Stevens looked at his watch.

'I've got baggage too,' he said, 'a valise and a kit bag

and some other junk. Perhaps you're right, Brian, and I'd do well to accompany you. Anyway it would halve the taxi fare.'

He rose from the table.

'Then I'll be bidding you all goodbye,' he said.

'Do you really have to go?' said Mrs Maclintick. 'We're just beginning to get to know you. Are you annoyed about something, like the girl you were with?'

In the course of her life she could rarely have gone further towards making an effort to show herself agreeable. It was a triumph for Stevens. He laughed, conscious of this, pleased at his success.

'Duty calls,' he said. 'I only wish I could stay till four in the morning, but they're beginning to shut down here as it is, even if I hadn't a train to catch.'

We said goodbye to him.

'Wonderful to have met you, Mr Moreland,' said Stevens. 'Here's to the next performance of *Vieux Port* on the same programme as your newest work—and may I be there to hear. Goodbye, Nicholas.'

He held out his hand. From being very sure of himself, he had now reverted a little to that less absolute confidence of the days when I had first known him. He was probably undecided as to the most effective note to strike in taking leave of us. It may at last have dawned on him that all the business of Priscilla could include embarrassments of a kind to which he had hitherto given little or no thought. The hesitation he showed possibly indicated indecision as to whether or not he should make further reference to her sudden withdrawal from the party. If, for a second, he had contemplated speaking of that, he must have changed his mind.

'We'll be meeting again,' he said.

'Goodbye.'

'And Happy Landings.'

'Come on, Odo, you oaf,' said the red-faced captain, 'cut out the fond farewells, or there won't be a cab left on the street. We've got to get cracking. Don't forget there'll be all that waffle with the RTO.'

They went off together, slapping each other on the back. 'He's a funny boy,' said Mrs Maclintick.

Stevens had made an impression on her. There could be no doubt of that. The way she spoke showed it. Although his presence that night had been unwelcome to myself—and the other two at first had also displayed no great wish to have him at the table—a distinct sense of flatness was discernible now Stevens was gone. Even Moreland, who had fidgeted when Mrs Maclintick had expressed regrets at this departure, seemed aware that the conviviality of the party was reduced by his removal. I said I should have to be making for bed.

'Oh, God, don't let's break it all up at once,' Moreland said. 'We've only just met. Those others prevented our talking of any of the things we really want to discuss—like the meaning of art, or how to get biscuits on the black market.'

'They won't serve any more drink here.'

'Come back to our place for a minute or two. There might be some beer left. We'll get old Max out of bed. He loves a gossip.'

'All right—but not for long.'

We paid the bill, went out into Regent Street. In the utter blackness, the tarts, strange luminous form of nocturnal animal life, flickered the bulbs of their electric torches. From time to time one of them would play the light against her own face in self-advertisement, giving the effect of candles illuminating a holy picture in the shadows of a church.

'Ingenious,' said Moreland.

'Don't doubt Maclintick would have found it so,' said Mrs Maclintick, not without bitterness.

A taxi set down its passengers nearby. We secured it. Moreland gave the address of the flat where he used to live with Matilda.

'I've come to the conclusion the characteristic women most detest in a man is unselfishness,' he said.

This remark had no particular bearing on anything that had gone before, evidently giving expression only to one of his long interior trains of thought.

'They don't have to put up with much of it,' said Mrs Maclintick. 'It's passed me by these forty years, but perhaps I'm lucky.'

'How their wives must have hated those saintly kings in the Middle Ages,' Moreland said. 'Still, as you truly remark, Audrey, one's speaking rather academically.'

The taxi had already driven off, and Moreland was putting the key in the lock of the front-door of the house, when the Air-raid Warning began to sound.

'Just timed it nicely,' Moreland said. 'That's the genuine article, not like the faint row when we were at dinner. No doubt at all allowed to remain in the mind. Are the flat's curtains drawn? I was the last to leave and it's the sort of thing I always forget to do.'

'Max will have fixed them,' said Mrs Maclintick.

We climbed the stairs, of which there were a great number, as they occupied the top floor flat.

'I hope Max is all right,' she said. 'I never like the idea of him being out in a raid. There's bound to be trouble if he spends the night in a shelter. He's always talking about giving the Underground a try-out, but I tell him I won't have him doing any such thing.'

If Moreland was one of Mrs Maclintick's children, clearly Max Pilgrim was another. We entered the flat behind her. Moreland did not turn on the switch until it was confirmed all windows were obscured. In the light, the apartment was revealed as untidier than in Matilda's day, otherwise much the same in outward appearance and decoration.

'Max . . .' shouted Mrs Maclintick.

She uttered this call from the bedroom. A faint answering cry came from another room further up the short passage. Its message was indeterminate, the tone, high and tremulous, bringing back echoes of a voice that had twittered through myriad forgotten night-clubs in the small hours.

'We've got a visitor, Max,' shouted Mrs Maclintick again.

'I hope there'll turn out to be some beer left,' said Moreland. 'I don't feel all that sure.'

He went into the kitchen. I remained in the passage. A door slowly opened at the far end. Max Pilgrim appeared, a tall willowy figure in horn-rimmed spectacles and a green brocade dressing gown. It was years since I had last seen him, where, I could not even remember, whether in the distance at a party, or, less likely, watching his act at some cabaret show. For a time he had shared a flat with Isobel's brother, Hugo, but we had not been in close touch with Hugo at that period, and had, as it happened, never visited the place. There had been talk of Pilgrim giving up his performances in those days and joining Hugo in the decorating business. Even at that time, Pilgrim's songs had begun to 'date', professionally speaking. However, that project had never come off, and, whatever people might say about being old-fashioned, Pilgrim continued to find himself in demand right up to the outbreak of war. Now, of course, he expressed to audiences all that was most nostalgic. Although his hair was dishevelled—perhaps because of that—he looked at this very moment as if about to break into one of his songs. He moved a little way up the passage, then paused.

'Here you are at last, my dears,' he said. 'You don't know how glad I am to see you. You must forgive what I'm looking like, which must be a perfect sight. I took off my slap before going to bed and am presenting you with a countenance natural and unadorned, something I'm always most unwilling to do.'

He certainly appeared pale as death. I had thought at first he was merely looking much older than I remembered. Now I accepted as explanation what he had said about lack of make-up. I noticed, too, that his right hand was bandaged. The voice was fainter than usual. He looked uncertainly at me, disguised in uniform. I explained I was Hugo's brother-in-law; that we had met once or twice in the past. Pilgrim took my right hand in his left.

'My dear . . .'

'How are you?'

'I've been having a most unenjoyable evening,' he said.

He did not at once release my hand. For some reason I felt a sudden lack of ease, an odd embarrassment, even apprehension, although absolutely accustomed to the rather unduly fervent social manner he was employing. I tried to withdraw from his grasp, but he held on tenaciously, almost as if he were himself requiring actual physical support.

154

'We hoped you were coming on from the Madrid to join us at dinner,' I said. 'Hugh tells me you were doing some of the real old favourites there.'

'I was.'

'Did you leave the Madrid too late?'

Then Max Pilgrim let go my hand. He folded his arms. His eyes were fixed on me. Although no longer linked to him by his own grasp, I continued to feel indefinably uncomfortable.

'You knew the Madrid?' he asked.

'I've been there—not often.'

'But enjoyed yourself there?'

'Always.'

'You'll never do that again.'

'Why not?'

'The Madrid is no more,' he said.

'Finished?'

'Finished.'

'The season or just your act?'

'The place—the building—the tables and chairs—the dance-floor—the walls—the ceiling—all those gold pillars. A bomb hit the Madrid full pitch this evening.'

'Max . . .'

Mrs Maclintick let out a cry. It was a reasonable moment to give expression to a sense of horror. Moreland had come into the passage from the kitchen, carrying a bottle of beer and three glasses. He stood for a moment, saying nothing; then we all went into the sitting-room. Pilgrim at once took the armchair. He nursed his bound hand, rocking himself slowly forward and back.

'In the middle of my act,' he said. 'It was getting the bird in a big way. Never experienced the like before, even on tour.'

'So there *was* a blitz earlier in the evening,' said Moreland.

'There was,' said Pilgrim. 'There certainly was.'

No one spoke for some seconds. Pilgrim continued to sit in the chair, looking straight in front of him, holding his wounded hand with the other. I knew there was a question I ought to ask, but felt almost physically inhibited from forming the words. In the end, Mrs Maclintick, not myself, put the enquiry.

'Anybody killed?'

Pilgrim nodded.

'Many?'

Pilgrim nodded again.

'Helped to get some of them out,' he said.

'There were a lot?'

'Of course it's a ghastly muddle on these occasions,' he said. 'Frenzied. Like Dante's Inferno. All in the black-out too. The wardens and I carried out six or seven at least. Must have. They'd all had it. I knew some of them personally. Nasty business, I can assure you. I suppose a few got away with it—like myself. They tried to persuade me to go with them and have some treatment, but after I'd had my hand bound up, all I wanted was home, sweet home. It's only a scratch, so I came back and tucked up. But I'm glad you're all here. Very glad.'

There was no escape now. So far as possible, certainty had to be established. An effort must be made.

'Bijou Ardglass was there with a party.'

Pilgrim looked at me with surprise.

'You knew that?' he said.

'Yes.'

'Were you asked? If so, you were lucky to have another engagement.'

'They were—'

'Bijou's table was just where it came through the ceiling.'

'So—'

'I'm afraid it was Bijou's last party.'

Pilgrim glanced away, quickly passing the bandaged hand across his eyes. It was an instinctive, not in the least dramatised, gesture.

'But the rest of them?'

'No one survived from that corner. That was where the worst of the damage was done. My end of the room wasn't so bad. That's why I'm here now.'

'You're sure all the Ardglass party—'

'They were the ones I helped carry out,' said Pilgrim. He spoke quite simply.

'Chips Lovell—'

'He'd been at the table.'

Moreland looked across at me. Mrs Maclintick took Pilgrim's arm.

'How did you get back yourself, Max?' she asked.

'I got a lift on one of the fire-engines. Can you imagine?'

'Here,' said Moreland. 'Have some beer.'

Pilgrim took the glass.

'I'd known Bijou for years,' he said. 'Known her when she was a little girl with a plait trying to get a job in the chorus. Wasn't any good for some reason. Can't think why, because she had the Theatre in her blood both sides. Do you know, Bijou's father played Abanazar in *Aladdin* when my mother was Principal Boy in the same show? Anyway, it all turned out best for Bijou in the end. Did much better as a mannequin than she'd ever have done on the boards. Met richer men, for one thing.'

There was a pause. Moreland cleared his throat uncomfortably. Mrs Maclintick sniffed. In the far distance, un-expectedly soon, the All Clear droned. It was followed, an instant later, by a more local siren.

'That one didn't take long,' Moreland said.

'Another tip-and-run raider,' said Pilgrim. 'The fashion of the moment.'

'It was a single plane caught the Madrid?'

'That's it.'

'I'll make some tea,' said Mrs Maclintick. 'Do us good.'

'Just what I need, Audrey, my dear,' said Pilgrim, sigh-ing. 'I couldn't think what it was. Now I know it's tea—not beer at all.'

He drank the beer all the same. Mrs Maclintick went off to the kitchen. It became clear that an unpleasant duty must be performed. There was no avoiding it. Priscilla would have to be told about the Madrid as soon as possible. If I called up the Jeavonses' house right away, the tele-phone, with any luck, would be answered by Molly Jeavons herself. I could tell her what had happened. She could break the news. So far as that went, even to make the announcement to Molly would be bad enough. It might be hard on her to have to tell Priscilla, but at least Molly was, by universal consent, a person adapted by nature to such harrowing tasks; warm-hearted, not over sensitive, grasping immediately the needs of the bereaved, saying just what was required, emotional yet never in-capacitated by emotion. Molly, if I were lucky, would do the job. There was always the chance Priscilla herself might be at the other end of the line. That was a risk that had to be taken into consideration. In a cowardly way, I delayed action until Mrs Maclintick had returned with the tea. After finishing a cup, I asked if I might use the tele-phone.

'By the bed,' said Moreland.

Pilgrim began to muse aloud.

'Strange those young Germans up there trying to kill me,' he murmured to himself. 'Ungrateful too. I've always had such good times in Berlin.'

The bedroom was more untidy than would ever have been allowed in Matilda's day. I sat on the edge of the bed and dialled the Jeavons number. There was no buzz. I tried again. After several unsuccessful attempts, none of which even achieved the 'number unobtainable' sound, I rang the Exchange. There were further delays. Then the operator tried the Jeavons number. That, too, was unproductive. No sound of ringing came. The line was out of order. I gave it up and returned to the sitting room.

'I can't get through. I'll have to go.'

'Stay the night, if you like,' said Mrs Maclintick. 'You can sleep on the sofa. Maclintick often did in our Pimlico place. Spent almost more time there than he did in bed.'

The offer was unexpected, rather touching in the circumstances. I saw she was probably able to look after Moreland better than I thought.

'No—thanks all the same. As I failed on the telephone, I'll have to go in person.'

'Priscilla?' said Moreland.

'Yes.'

He nodded.

'What a job,' he said.

Max Pilgrim gathered his dressing gown round him. He yawned and stretched.

'I wonder when the next one will arrive,' he said. 'Worse than waiting for the curtain to go up.'

I said goodnight to them. Moreland came to the door.

'I suppose you've really got to do this?' he said.

'Not much avoiding it.'

'Glad it's not me,' he said.

'You're right to be.'

There seemed no more taxis left in London. I walked for a time, then, totally unlooked for at that hour, a bus stopped by the place I was passing. Without any very clear idea of doing more than move in a south-westerly direction, I boarded it, in this way travelled as far as a stop in the neighbourhood of Gloucester Road. Here the journey had to be resumed on foot. The pavements were endless, threading a way down them like those interminable rovings pursued in dreams. Cutting through several side turnings, I at last found myself among a conjunction of dark red brick Renaissance-type houses. In one of these the Jeavonses had lived for twenty years or more, an odd centre of miscellaneous hospitality to which Chips Lovell himself had first taken me. In the lower reaches of their street, two fire-engines were drawn up. By the light of electric torches, firemen and air-raid wardens were passing in and out of one of the front-doors. This particular house turned out to be the Jeavonses'. In the dark, little was to be seen of what was happening. Apart from these dim figures going to and fro, like the trolls in *Peer Gynt*, nothing seemed abnormal about the façade. There was no sign of damage to the structure. One of the wardens, in helmet and overalls, stopped by the steps and lit a cigarette.

'Did this house get it?'

'About an hour ago,' he said, 'that last tip-and-run raider.'

'Anybody hurt?'

He took the cigarette from his mouth and nodded.

'I know the people—are they about?'

'You know Mr Jeavons and Lady Molly?'

'Yes.'

'You've only just arrived here?'

'That's it.'

'Mr Jeavons and me are on the same warden-post,' he said. 'They've taken him down there. Giving him a cup of tea.'

'Was he injured?'

'It was her.'

'Badly?'

The warden looked at me as if I should not have asked that question.

'You hadn't heard?' he said.

'No.'

'Didn't survive.'

He went on speaking at once, as if from a kind of embarrassment at having to announce such a thing.

'She and the young lady,' he said. 'It was all at the back of the house. You wouldn't think there was a jot of damage out here in front, but there's plenty inside, I can tell you. Dreadful thing. Used to see a lot of them. Always very friendly people. Got their newspapers from me, matter of fact. If you know them, there's a lady inside can tell you all about it.'

'I'll go in.'

He threw away the stub of his cigarette and trod on it.

'So long,' he said.

'So long.'

He was right about there being a mess inside. A woman in some sort of uniform was giving instructions to the people clearing up. She turned out to be Eleanor Walpole-Wilson.

'Eleanor.'

She looked round.

'Hullo, Nick,' she said. 'Thank goodness you've come.'

She did not seem at all surprised to see me. She came across the hall. Now in her middle thirties, Eleanor was less unusual in appearance than as a girl. No doubt uniform suited her. Though her size and shape had also become more conventional, she retained an air of having been never properly assimilated to either sex. At the same time, big and broad-shouldered, she was not exactly a 'mannish' woman. Her existence might have been more viable had that been so.

'You've heard what's happened?' she said abruptly.

Her manner, too, so out of place in ordinary social relations, had equally come into its own.

'Molly's . . .'

'And Priscilla.'

'God.'

'One of the Polish officers too—the nice one. The other's pretty well all right, just a bang over the head. That wretched girl who got into trouble with the Norwegian has been taken to hospital. She'll be all right, too, when she's recovered from the shock. I don't know whether she'll keep the baby.'

It was clear all this briskness was specifically designed to carry Eleanor through. She must have been having a very bad time indeed.

'A man at the door—one of the wardens—said Ted was down at the post.'

'He was there when it happened. They may have taken him on to the hospital by now. How did you hear about it? I didn't know you were in London.'

'I'm passing through on leave.'

'Is Isobel all right?'

'She's all right. She's in the country.'

Just for the moment I felt unable to explain anything very lucidly, to break through the barricade of immediate action and rapid talk with which Eleanor was protecting herself. It was like trying to tackle her in the old days, when she had been training one of her dogs with a whistle, and would not listen to other people round her. She must have developed early in life this effective method of shutting herself off from the rest of the world; a weapon, no doubt, against parents and early attempts to make her live a conventional sort of life. Now, while she talked, she continued to move about the hall, clearing up some of the debris. She was wearing a pair of green rubber gloves that made me think of the long white ones she used to draw on at dances.

'We shall have to have a talk as to who must be told about all this—and in what order. Are you in touch with Chips?'

'Eleanor—Chips has been killed too.'

Eleanor stopped her tidying up. I told her what had happened at the Madrid. She began to take off the green gloves. People were passing through the passage all the time. Eleanor put the rubber gloves on the top of the marquetry cabinet Molly's sister had left her when she died, the one Ted Jeavons had never managed to move out of the hall.

'Let's go upstairs and sit down for a bit,' she said. 'I've had just about as much as I can take. We can sit in the drawing room. That was one of the rooms that came off least badly.'

We went up to the first floor. The drawing room, thick in dust and fallen plaster, had a long jagged fissure down one wall. There were two rectangular discoloured spaces where the Wilson and the Greuze had hung. These pictures had presumably been removed to some safer place at the outbreak of war. So, too, had a great many of the oriental bowls and jars that had formerly played such a part in the decoration. They might have been valuable or absolute rubbish; Lovell had always insisted the latter. The pastels, by some unknown hand, of Moroccan types remained. They were hanging at all angles, the glass splintered of one bearing the caption *Rainy Day at Marrakesh*. Eleanor and I sat on the sofa. She began to cry.

'It's all too awful,' she said, 'and I was so fond of Molly. You know, she usen't to like me. When Norah and I first shared a flat together, Molly didn't approve. She put out a story I wore a green pork-pie hat and a bow tie. It wasn't true. I never did. Anyway, why shouldn't I, if I wanted to? There I was in the country breeding labradors and bored to death, and all my parents wanted was for me to get married, which I hadn't the least wish to do. Norah came to stay and suggested I should join her in taking a flat. There it was. Norah was always quite good at getting jobs in shops and that sort of thing, and I found all the stuff I knew about dogs could be put to some use too when it came to the point. Besides, I'd always adored Norah.'

I had sometimes wondered how Eleanor's ménage with Norah Tolland had begun. No one ever seemed to know. Now it was explained.

'Where's Norah now?'

'In Scotland, driving for the Poles.'

She dried her eyes.

'Come on,' she said. 'We must get out some sort of plan. No good just sitting about. I'll find a pencil and paper.'

She began to rummage in one of the drawers.

'Here we are.'

We made lists of names, notes of things that would have to be done. One of the wardens came up to say that for the time being the house was safe to stay in, they were going home.

'Where are you spending the night, Nick?'

'A club.'

'There might be someone who could take you part of the way. The chief warden's got a car.'

'What about you?'

'I shall be all right. There's a room fitted up with a bed in the basement. Ted used it sometimes, if he had to come in very late.'

'Will you really be all right?'

She dismissed the question of herself rather angrily. The ARP official with the car was found.

'Goodbye, Eleanor.'

I kissed her, which I had never done before.

'Goodbye, Nick. Love to Isobel. It was lucky I was staying here really, because there'll be a lot that will have to be done.'

The fire-engines had driven away. The street was empty. I thought how good Eleanor was in a situation like this. Molly had been good, too, when it came to disaster. I wondered what would happen to Ted. The extraordinary thing about the outside of the house was that everything looked absolutely normal. Some sort of a notice about bomb damage had been stuck on the front-door by the wardens; otherwise there was nothing to indicate the place had been subjected to an attack from the air, which had killed several persons. This lack of outward display was comparable with the Madrid's fate earlier that evening, when a lot of talking in a restaurant had been sufficient to drown the sound of the Warning, the noise of the guns.

This must be what Dr Trelawney called 'the slayer of Osiris and his grievous tribute of blood'. I wondered if Dr Trelawney himself had survived: when Odo Stevens would receive the news: whether the Lovells' daughter, Caroline, would be brought up by her grandparents. Reflecting on these things, it did not seem all that long time ago that Lovell, driving back from the film studios in that extraordinary car of his, had suggested we should look in on the Jeavonses', because 'the chief reason I want to visit Aunt Molly is to take another look at Priscilla Tolland, who is quite often there.'

3

THE FIRST MEAL EATEN IN Mess after return from leave is always dispiriting. Room, smell, food, company, at first seemed unchanged; as ever, unenchanting. On taking a seat at table I remembered with suddenly renewed sense of internal discomfort that Stringham would be on duty. In the pressure of other things that had been happening, I had forgotten about him. However, when the beef appeared, it was handed round by a red-haired gangling young soldier with a hare-lip and stutter. There was no sign of Stringham. The new waiter could be permanent, or just a replacement imported to F Mess while Stringham himself was sick, firing a musketry course, temporarily absent for some other routine reason. Opportunity to enquire why he was gone, at the same time to betray no exceptional interest in him personally, arose when Soper complained of the red-haired boy's inability to remember which side of the plate, as a matter of common practice, were laid knife, fork and spoon.

'Like animals, some of them,' Soper said. 'As for getting a message delivered, you're covered with spit before he's halfway through.'

'What happened to the other one?'

If asked a direct question of that sort, Soper always looked suspicious. Finding, after a second or two, no grounds for imputing more than idle curiosity to this one, he returned a factual, though reluctant, reply.

'Went to the Mobile Laundry.'

'For the second time of asking, Soper,' said Macfie, 'will you pass the water jug?'

'Here you are, Doc. Those tablets come in yet?'

Macfie was gruff about the tablets, Soper persuasive. The Cipher Officer remarked on the amount of flu about. There was general agreement, followed by some discussion of prevalent symptoms. The subject of Stringham had to be started up again from scratch.

'Did you sack him?'

'Sack who?'

'The other Mess waiter.'

'What's he got to do with you?'

'Just wondered.'

'He was transferred to the Laundry from one day to the next. Bloody inconvenient for this Mess. He'd have done the job all right if Biggy hadn't been on at him all the time. I complained to the DAAG about losing a waiter like that, but he said it had got to go through.'

Biggs, present at table, but in one of his morose moods that day, neither denied nor confirmed his own part in the process of Stringham's dislodgement. He chewed away at a particularly tough piece of meat, looking straight in front of him. Soper, as if Biggs himself were not sitting there, continued to muse on the aversion felt by Biggs for Stringham.

'That chap drove Biggy crackers for some reason,' he said. 'Something about him. Wasn't only the way he talked. Certainly was a dopey type. Don't know how he got where he was. Had some education. I could see that. You'd think he'd have found better employment than a Mess waiter. Got a bad record, I expect. Trouble back in Civvy Street.'

That Stringham had himself engineered an exchange from F Mess to avoid relative persecution at the hands of Biggs was, I thought, unlikely. In his relationship with Biggs, even a grim sort of satisfaction to Stringham might be suspected, one of those perverse involutions of feeling that had brought him into the army in the first instance. Such sentiments were hard to unravel. They were perhaps no more tangled than the rest of the elements that made up Stringham's life—or anybody else's life when closely examined. Not only had he disregarded loopholes which invited avoidance of the Services—health, and, at that period, age too—but, in face of much apparent discouragement from the recruiting authorities, had shown uncharacteristic persistence to get where he was. One aspect of this determination to carry through the project of joining the army was no doubt an attempt to rescue a self-respect badly battered during the years with Miss Weedon; however much she might also have accomplished in setting Stringham on his feet. An innate restlessness certainly played a part too; taste for change, even for adventure of a sort; all perhaps shading off into a vague romantic patriotism that especially allured by its own ironic connotations, its very lack, so to speak, of what might be called contemporary intellectual prestige.

'Awfully chic to be killed,' he had said.

Death was a prize, at least on the face of it, that war always offered. Lovell's case had demonstrated how the unexpected could happen within a few hours to those who deplored a sedentary job. Thinking over Stringham's more immediate situation, it seemed likely that, hearing of a vacancy in the ranks of the Mobile Laundry, he had decided on impulse to explore a new, comparatively exotic field of army life in his self-imposed military pilgrimage. Bithel could even have marked down Stringham as a man likely to do credit to the unit he commanded. That, I decided, was even more probable. These speculations had taken place during one of the Mess's long silences, less nerve-racking than those at the general's table, but also, in most respects, even more dreary. Biggs suddenly, unexpectedly, returned to the subject.

'Glad that bugger's gone,' he said. 'Got me down. It's a fact he did. I've got worries enough as it is, without having him about the place.'

He spoke as if it were indeed a great relief to him. I had to admit to myself that Stringham's physical removal was a great relief to me too. This sense of deliverance, of moral alleviation, was at the same time tempered with more than a trace of guilt, because, so far as potential improvement in his state was in question, Stringham had left F Mess without the smallest assistance from myself. I dispelled such twinges of conscience by reflecting that the Mobile Laundry, at least while Bithel remained in command, led for the moment a raggle-taggle gipsy life, offering, at least on the face of it, a less thankless daily prospect than being a Mess waiter. If absorbed into the Divisional Concert Party, he might even bring off a vocalist's stage debut, something he used to talk of on the strength of having been briefly in the choir at school. In short, the problem seemed to me to resolve itself—after an honourable, even quixotic gesture on Stringham's part—to finding the least uncongenial niche available in the circumstances. That supposition was entirely my own. It was probably far removed from Stringham's personal ambitions, if these were at all formulated.

'What's on your mind, Biggy?' said Soper. 'You're not yourself today.'

'Oh, stuff it up,' said Biggs, 'I've got a pile of trouble. Those lawyers are going to skin me.'

When I saw Widmerpool that afternoon I spoke about Stringham going to the Mobile Laundry.

'It was my idea to send him there.'

'A very good one.'

'It seemed the solution.'

Widmerpool did not elaborate what he had done. I was surprised, rather impressed, by the speed with which he had taken action, especially after earlier remarks about leaving Stringham where he was. It looked as if Widmerpool had thought things over and decided there was something to be said for trying to make Stringham's existence more agreeable, however contrary that might be to a rule of life that taught disregard for the individual. I felt I had for once misjudged Widmerpool, too readily accepted the bleak façade displayed, which, anyway in Stringham's case, might screen a complex desire to conceal good nature, however intermittent.

General Liddament had to be faced on the subject of my own missed Free French opportunities. The matter was not one of sufficient importance—at the General's end —to ask for an interview through Greening, so I had to wait until the Divisional Commander was to be found alone. As I rarely saw him during daily routine, this took place once again on an exercise. Defence Platoon duties usually brought me to breakfast first on those mornings, even before Cocksidge, otherwise in the vanguard of the rest of the staff. The General varied in his habits, sometimes early, sometimes late. That morning, he had appeared at table before Cocksidge himself, who, as it turned out later, had been delayed by breaking a bootlace or cutting his rubber-like face shaving. When the General had drunk some tea, I decided to tackle him.

'I saw Major Finn in London, sir.'

'Finn?'

'Yes, sir.'

'How was he?'

'Very well, sir. Sent his respects. He said my French was not up to liaison work at battalion level.'

'Ah.'

That was General Liddament's sole comment. He drank more tea in huge gulps, while he studied a map. The fact that Cocksidge entered the room a minute or two later did not, I think, affect the conversation in any way; I mean so far as further discussion of my own affairs by the General might have taken place. That was already at an end. Cocksidge was quite overcome by finding the Divisional Commander already almost at the end of breakfast.

'Excuse me, sir,' he said, 'but I do believe they've given you the chipped cup. I'll change it at once, sir. I wonder how often I've spoken to the Mess Sergeant about that cup, sir, and told him never to give it to a senior officer, and above all not yourself, sir. I'll make sure it never happens again, sir.'

Military action in Syria had been making it clear why there had been call for more British liaison officers with the Free French overseas. I thought of the 9th Regiment of Colonial Infantry being harangued by someone with better command of the language—and more histrionic talent—than myself. Then the Germans attacked in Crete. The impression was that things were not going too well there. Meanwhile, the Division continued to train; policies, units, began to take more coherent shape, to harden: new weapons were issued: instructors improved. The Commanding Officer of the Reconnaissance Unit remained unappointed. I asked Widmerpool if he had progressed further in placing his own candidate. The question did not please him.

'Difficulties have arisen.'

'Someone else getting the command?'

'I can't quite understand what is happening,' said Widmerpool. 'There has been no opportunity to go into the matter lately. This Diplock case has been taking up so much of my time. The more I investigate, the more incriminated Diplock seems to be. There's going to be hell to pay. Hogbourne-Johnson is behaving very badly, making himself offensive to me personally, and doing his best to shield the man and cause obstruction. That is quite useless. I am confident I shall be able to show that Diplock's behaviour has been not merely irregular, but criminal. Pedlar is almost equally unwilling to believe the worst, but at least Pedlar approaches the matter with a reasonably open mind, even if a slow one.'

'Does the General know about Diplock?'

'Hogbourne-Johnson says there is not sufficient evidence yet to lay before him.'

In the matter of Diplock, I believed Widmerpool to be on the right track. Few things are more extraordinary in human behaviour than the way in which old sweats like this chief clerk Warrant Officer will suddenly plunge into serious misdoing—usually on account of a woman. Diplock might well have a career of petty dishonesty behind him, but this looked like something far more serious.

'Talking of the Recce Unit,' said Widmerpool, 'there's still some sorting out to be done about the officer establishment. At least one of the captaincies assigned to that unit, before it came into existence, is still—owing to some whim of the General's—in use elsewhere as a local rank. That is one of the things I want you to go into among the stuff I am leaving tonight.'

'Establishments without troops always make one think of *Dead Souls*. A military Chichikov could first collect battalions, then brigades, finally a Division—and be promoted major-general.'

I said that to tease Widmerpool, feeling pretty certain he had never read a line of Gogol, though he would rarely if ever admit to failure in recognising an allusion, literary or otherwise. On this occasion he merely nodded his head several times; then returned to the fact that, contrary to his usual practice, he would not be working after dinner that evening.

'For once I shall cut office hours tonight,' he said. 'I'm giving dinner to that fellow—for the moment his name escapes me—from the Military Secretary's branch, who is doing a tour of duty over here.'

'Is this in the interests of the Recce Unit appointment?'

Widmerpool winked, a habit of his only when in an exceptionally good temper.

'More important than that,' he said.

'Yourself?'

'Dinner may put the finishing touches to something.'

'Promotion?'

'Who knows? It's been in the air for some time, as a matter of fact.'

Widmerpool rarely allowed himself a night off in this manner. He worked like an automaton. Work, civil or military, was his sole interest. If it came to that, he never gave his assistant a night off either, if he could help it, because everyone who served under him was expected to do so to the fullest extent of his powers, which was no doubt reasonable enough. The result was that a great deal of work was completed in the DAAG's office, some useful, some less useful. On the whole the useful work, it had to be admitted, made up for a fair percentage of time and energy wasted on Widmerpool's pet projects, of which there were several. I was thinking of such things while stowing away papers in the safe that night, preparatory to leaving Headquarters for bed. I shut the safe and locked it. The time was ten o'clock or thereabouts. The telephone bell began to ring.

'DAAG's office.'

'Nick?'

The voice was familiar. All the same, I could not immediately place it. No officer at Div HQ used just that intimate inflexion when pronouncing my name.

'Speaking.'

'It's Charles.'

That took me no further. So far as I could remember, none of the local staff were called 'Charles'. It must be someone recently arrived in the place, who knew me.

'Charles who?'

'Private Stringham, sir—pardon the presumption.'

'Charles—yes—sorry.'

'Bit of luck catching you in.'

'I'm just leaving, as a matter of fact. How did you know I was here?'

'I rang up F Mess first—in the character of General Fauncefoot-Fritwell's ADC.'

'Who on earth is General Fauncefoot-Fritwell?'

'Just a name that occurred to me as belonging to the sort of officer of senior rank who would own an ADC—so

175

don't worry if Captain Biggs, who I think answered the telephone, mentions the General to you. He will say there was no message. Captain Biggs, if it was indeed he, sounded quite impressed, even rather frightened. He told me you were probably still working, unless on your way back now. I must say, you officers are kept at it.'

'But, Charles, what is all this about?'

I thought he must be drunk, and began to wonder how best to deal with him. This was just the sort of embarrassment Widmerpool had envisaged. It could be awkward. I experienced one of those moments—they cropped up from time to time—of inwardly agreeing there was something to be said for Widmerpool's point of view. However Stringham sounded perfectly sober; though to sound sober was not unknown as one of the characteristics he was apt to display after a great deal to drink. That was especially true of the period immediately preceding his going under entirely. I felt apprehensive.

'Yes, I must come to the point, Nick,' he said. 'I'm getting dreadfully garrulous in old age. It's barrack-room life. Look, forgive me for ringing up at this late hour, which I know to be contrary to good order and discipline. The fact is I find myself with a problem on my hands.'

'What's happened?'

'You know my officer, Mr Bithel?'

'Of course.'

'You will therefore be aware that—like my former unregenerate self—he is at times what our boyhood's mentor, Mr Le Bas, used to call a devotee of Bacchus?'

'Bithel's drunk?'

'Got it in one. Rather overdone the Dionysian rites.'

'Passed out?'

'Precisely.'

'Whereabouts?'

'I've just tripped over his prostrate form on the way back to bed. When I was suddenly, quite unexpectedly, whisked away from F Mess, and enlisted under Mr Bithel's gallant command, he behaved very kindly to me on arrival. He has done so ever since. I therefore feel grateful towards him. I thought—to avoid further danger to himself, physical or moral—you might have some idea of the best way of getting him back without undue delay to wherever he belongs. Otherwise some interfering policeman, civil or military, will feel it his duty to put the Lieutenant in the cooler. I'm not sure where he's housed. G Mess, is it? Anyway, I can't manage him all on my own-io, as the Edwardian song used to say. I wondered if you had any suggestions.'

This emergency had noticeably cheered Stringham. That was plain, even on the telephone. There was only one thing to do.

'I'll come along. What about yourself? Are you all right for time?'

'I'm on a late pass.'

'And where are you exactly?'

Stringham described a spot not far from where we had met in the street on that earlier occasion. The place was about ten minutes' walk from Headquarters; rather more from G Mess, where Bithel slept.

'I'll stand guard over Mr B. until you arrive,' Stringham said. 'At the moment he's propped up out of harm's way on the steps of a bombed house. Bring a torch, if you've got one. It's as dark as hell and stinks of something far worse than cheese.'

By some incredibly lucky concatenation of circumstances, Bithel had managed, though narrowly, to escape court-martial over the affair of the bouncing cheque that had worried him the night of the biggish raid of several weeks before. However, Widmerpool had now stated categorically he was on the point of removing Bithel from the Mobile Laundry command as soon as he could negotiate that matter satisfactorily with the authority to whom the Laundry was ultimately responsible. That might be a judgment from which there was no appeal, but, even so, gave no reason to deny a hand in getting Bithel as far as his own bed that night, rather than leave him to be picked up by the Provost Marshal or local constabulary. It was even possible that definite official notification of his final sacking might have brought about this sudden alcoholic downfall; until now kept by Bithel within reasonable bounds. He would certainly be heartbroken at losing the command of the Mobile Laundry, of which he was, indeed, said to have made a fair success. If this intimation had reached him, he might be additionally upset because dismissal would almost certainly mark the first stage of final ejection from the army. Bithel was proud of being in the army; it also brought him a livelihood. Apart from any of that, Stringham had to be backed up in undertaking Bithel's rescue. That was how things looked. I made a last inspection of the office to make sure no papers had been left outside the safe that should have been locked away, then left Headquarters.

Outside in the street, it was impossible to see a yard ahead without a torch. In spite of that, I found the place without much difficulty. Stringham, hands in his pockets, was leaning against the wall of a house that had been burnt out by an incendiary bomb a week or two before. He was smoking a cigarette.

'Hullo, Nick.'

'Where's Bithel?'

'At the top of these steps. I pulled him up there out of the way. He seemed to be coming-to a moment ago. Then he sank back again. Let's go and have a look at him.'

Bithel was propped up under a porch against the front-door of the house, his legs stretched down the steps, head sunk on one shoulder. This was all revealed by a flash of the torch. He was muttering a little to himself. We examined him.

'Where's he got to go?' asked Stringham.

'G Mess. That's not too far from here.'

'Can we carry him feet first?'

'Not a very tempting prospect in the blackout. Can't we wake him up and force him to walk? Everyone must realize they have to make a special effort in wartime. Why should Bithel be absolved from that?'

'How severe you always are to human weakness, Nick.'

We shook Bithel, who was again showing slight signs of revival, at least in so much that protests were wrung from him by this rough treatment.

'. . . Don't shake us, old man . . . don't shake us like that . . . whatever are you doing it for? . . . makes me feel awful . . . I'll throw up . . . I will really . . .'

'Bith, you've got to pull yourself together, get back to your billet.'

'What's that you're saying . . .'

'Can you stand up? If so, we'll hold you on either side.'

'. . . Can't remember your name, old man . . . didn't see you in that last pub . . . couldn't see any officers there . . . rather glad of that . . . prefer talking to those young fellows without a lot of majors poking their noses in . . . keep in touch with the men . . . never go far wrong if you do that . . . take an interest in them off duty . . . then it got late . . . couldn't find the way home . . .'

'It *is* late, Bith. That's why we've got to take you back to bed. It's Nick Jenkins. We're going to pilot you to G Mess.'

'Nick Jenkins . . . in the Regiment together. . . . Do you remember . . . *Mr Vice—the Loyal Toast* . . . then, you . . .'

'That's it.'

'*The King* . . .'

Bithel shouted the words, turning on one elbow and making as if to raise a glass in the air.

'*The King*, Bith.'

'Loved the old Regiment. . . . Give you *The Regiment* . . . no heelers. . . . Age shall not . . . something . . . nor the years condemn . . .'

'Come on, Bith, make an effort.'

'. . . at the going down of the sun . . . that's it . . . we shall remember them . . .'

He suddenly began to sing in a thin piping voice, not unlike Max Pilgrim's.

'Fol-low, fol-low, we will fol-low Davies—
    We will follow Davies, everywhere he leads . . .'

'Bith.'

'Remember how we went romping all over the house that Christmas night after dinner . . . when the Mess was in those former bank premises . . . trailing along behind Colonel Davies . . . under the tables . . . over the chairs . . . couldn't do it this moment for five pounds . . . God, I do really believe I'm going to throw up . . .'

We got him to his feet with a tremendous heave. This

sudden change of posture was too much for Bithel, who had rightly judged his own digestive condition. After much vomiting, he seemed appreciably more sober. We had allowed him to sink on all fours to the ground while relieving his stomach. Now we raised him again on his feet to prepare for the journey back to G Mess.

'If you can walk, Bith, we'll take you home now. Stringham, one of your own chaps, is here to help.'

'String . . .'

'Here, sir,' said Stringham, who had begun to laugh a lot. 'Stringham of the Mobile Laundry, present and correct.'

The name, coupled with that of his command, faintly animated Bithel. Perhaps it suggested to him the title of one of those adventure stories he had enjoyed as a boy; certainly the picaresque operation of a Mobile Laundry would have made an enthralling Henty volume.

'That 'varsity man the DAAG sent to me?'

'That's the one, sir.'

'Only good turn Major Widmerpool's ever done me . . .'

Stringham was now laughing so much we had to lower Bithel to the ground again.

'I know just how you're feeling, sir,' said Stringham. 'Nobody better.'

'Stringham's a 'varsity man, like yourself, Nick. . . . Did you know that? . . . good type . . . got some fine boys in the Laundry . . . proud to command them . . . Sergeant Ablett . . . splendid type. . . . You should hear him sing *The Man who broke the Bank at Monte Carlo* . . . brings back the old music halls . . . but Stringham's the only 'varsity man . . .'

The access of emotion that had now descended on Bithel was in danger of changing once more to stupor. He began to breathe heavily. We tried to lift him again from the pavement.

'One of the things I like about him,' said Stringham, 'is the fact there's so little difference when he's sober. Drink doesn't make him turn nasty. On the contrary. How well one knows the feeling of loving the whole world after downing a few doubles. As I no longer drink, I no longer love the whole world—nor, if it comes to that, even a small part of it.'

'All the same, you took the trouble to be a Good Samaritan on this occasion.'

'After all, he is my Commanding Officer—and has been very gracious to me. I still have some gratitude, even if no general goodwill towards mankind. I like gratitude, because it's the rarest of virtues and a very difficult one to cultivate. For example, I never feel nearly grateful enough to Tuffy. In some respects, I'm ashamed to say I'm even conscious of a certain resentment towards her. Tonight's good deed was just handed me on a plate. Such a conscience have I now developed, I even feel grateful to Widmerpool. That does me credit, doesn't it? Do you know, Nick, he went out of his way to get me moved from F Mess to the Mobile Laundry—just as an act of pure kindness. Who'd have thought that of Widmerpool? I learnt the fact from Mr Bithel himself, who was equally surprised at the DAAG finding suitable personnel for him. I must say I was at once attracted by the idea of widening my military experience. Besides, there are some real treasures in the Laundry. I don't know how I can show Widmerpool gratitude. Keep out of the way, I suppose. The one thing I can't understand is Mr Bithel's obsession with university life. I explained to him, when he brought up the subject, that my own college days had been among the most melancholic of a life not untinged by shadow.'

All the time Stringham had been speaking, we were trying to galvanise Bithel from his spell of total collapse into a state of renewed awareness. We achieved this, finally bringing him into actual motion.

'Now, if you'll guide us, Nick, we'll have the Lieutenant tucked up between sheets in no time.'

Once we had Bithel traversing the pavement between us, the going was quite good in spite of Stygian darkness. In fact, we must have been within a hundred and fifty yards of G Mess before anything inopportune occurred. Then was disaster. The worst happened. Stringham and I were rounding a corner, Bithel mumbling incomprehensibly between us, when a figure, walking hurriedly from the other direction, collided violently with our party. The effect of this strong oncoming impact was for Stringham to let go of Bithel's arm, so that, taken by surprise and unable to support the full weight alone, I too became disengaged from Bithel, who sank heavily to the ground. The person who had obstructed us also stumbled and swore, a moment later playing a torch on my face, so that I could not see him or anything else.

'What the hell is happening?'

The voice was undoubtedly Widmerpool's, especially recognisable when angry. His quarters were also in this neighbourhood. He was on his way back to B Mess after dinner with his acquaintance from the Military Secretary's branch. This was a most unfortunate encounter. The only thing to do was to fabricate as quickly as possible some obvious excuse for Bithel's condition, and hope for the best.

'This officer must have tripped in the black-out,' I said.

'He had knocked himself out. We're taking him back to his billet.'

Widmerpool played his torch on each of us in turn.

'Nicholas . . .' he said, 'Bithel . . . Stringham . . .'

He spoke Stringham's name with surprise, not much approval. Since identities were now revealed, there was now no hope of proceeding without further explanation.

'Charles Stringham found Bithel lying stunned. He got in touch with me. We're taking him back to G Mess.'

That might have sounded reasonably convincing, if only Bithel himself had kept quiet. However, the last fall seemed, if not to have sobered him, at least to have shaken off the coma into which he had sunk at an earlier stage. Now, without any help from the rest of us, he picked himself up off the pavement. He took Widmerpool by the arm.

'Ought to go home . . .' he said. 'Ought to go home . . . had too much of that bloody porter . . . sickly stuff when you mix it with gin-and-italian . . . never do if we run into the APM . . .'

Then he began to sing again, though in a lower key than before.

'Fol-low, fol-low, we will follow Davies . . .'

The words of the rest of the song were drowned at that moment by the sudden note of the Air-raid Warning. For me, the ululating call registered a routine summons not to be disregarded. Bithel's troubles, however acute, must now be accepted as secondary to overseeing that the Defence Platoon reported for duty, without delay mounted their brens for aircraft action. A chance remained that this diversion might distract Widmerpool's attention from the business of getting Bithel home. There was no reason for Widmerpool to hang about in the streets after the Warning had gone. His orderly mind might indicate that correct procedure for him was to take shelter. However, he made no such move, only disengaging himself from Bithel by pushing him against the wall. He must have grasped the situation perfectly, seen at once that the first thing to do was to get Bithel himself out of the way. Certainly he retained no doubts as to why Bithel had been found lying on the pavement, but accepted at the same time the fact that there was no point in making a fuss then and there. Disciplinary action, if required, was to be attended to later. This was neither the time nor the place.

'I'll have to leave him on your hands now. I've got to get those bren posts distributed forthwith.'

'Yes, get off to the Defence Platoon right away,' said Widmerpool. 'Look sharp about it. Stringham and I will get this sot back to bed. I'll see this is the last time the army's troubled with him. It will only be a matter of expediting matters already in hand. Take one side, Stringham.'

Bithel was still leaning against the wall. Stringham once more took him by the arm. At the same time, he turned towards Widmerpool.

'It's interesting to recall, sir,' he said, 'the last time we met, I myself was the inert frame. It was you and Mr Jenkins who so kindly put me to bed. It shows that improvement is possible, that roles can be reversed. I've turned over a new leaf. Stringham is enrolled in the ranks of the sober, as well as the brave.'

I did not wait to hear Widmerpool's reply. The guns had started up. A helmet had to be collected before doing the rounds of the sections. After acquiring the necessary equipment, I set about my duties. The Defence Platoon got off the mark well that night.

'They always come a Wednesday,' said Sergeant Harmer. 'Might as well sit up for them.'

As blitzes went, that night's was not too bad a one. They went home early. We were in bed by half-past twelve.

'No more news about me, I suppose, sir?' asked Corporal Mantle, before he marched away his section.

I told him I would have another word with the DAAG. As it happened, the following morning had to be devoted to Defence Platoon affairs, so I did not see Widmerpool until the afternoon. I was not sorry about that, because it gave a time for cooling off. After the Bithel affair, an ill humour, even a downright row, was to be expected. However, this turned out to be a wrong appraisal. When I arrived in the room Widmerpool gave the impression of being more than usually pleased with himself. He pushed away the papers in front of him, evidently intending to speak at once of what had happened the night before, rather than get through the afternoon's routine, and institute a disagreeable post mortem on the subject at the end of the day's work, a rather favourite practice of his when he wanted to make a fuss about something.

'Well,' he said.

'Did you deal with Bithel?'

'I did.'

'What happened?'

I meant, by that question, to ask what had taken place over the next hundred yards or so of pavement leading to G Mess, how Bithel had been physically conveyed to his room. Widmerpool chose to understand the enquiry as referring to the final settlement of Bithel as a local problem.

'I had a word with A & Q this morning,' he said.

'Bithel's been sent on immediate leave. He will shortly be removed from the army.'

'By court-martial?'

'Unnecessary—purely administrative relegation to civilian life will save both time and trouble.'

'That can be done?'

'Bithel himself agrees it is the best way.'

'You've seen him?'

'I sent for him first thing this morning.'

'How was he feeling?'

'I have no idea. I am not concerned with the state of his health. I simply offered him the alternative of court-martial or acceptance of the appropriate report declaring him unsuitable for retention as an officer. The administrative documents releasing him from the army in the shortest possible period of time are now in motion. He wisely concurred, though not without an extraordinary scene.'

'What sort of scene?'

'Tears poured down his cheeks.'

'He was upset?'

'So it appeared.'

The episode plainly struck Widmerpool as of negative interest. That he should feel no pity for Bithel was reasonable enough, but it was a mark of his absolute lack of interest in human beings, as such, that the several implications of the interview—its sheer physical grotesqueness, for example, in the light of what Bithel must have drunk the night before—had made no impression on him he thought worth repeating. On the other hand, the clean-cut line of action he had taken emphasised his ability in dealing decisively with a problem of the kind Bithel raised by his very existence. Widmerpool's method was a contrast with that of my former Company Commander, Rowland Gwatkin, earlier confronted with Bithel in another of his unsatisfactory incarnations. When Bithel had drunk too much at the Castlemallock Gas School, Gwatkin had profitlessly put him under close arrest. Then he had omitted to observe the required formalities in relation to army arrest, with the result that the whole procedure collapsed. That, it was true, had not been entirely Gwatkin's fault; nevertheless, from Gwatkin's own point of view, the action had totally miscarried. With Widmerpool, on the other hand, there was no melodrama; only effective disposal of the body. The Bithel problem was at an end. If Bithel handicapped the war effort further, that would be in a civilian capacity.

'A pity the Warning went off like that last night,' said Widmerpool, speaking rather savagely. 'We could have frog-marched the brute back to his billet. I've seen it done with three.'

'Who will command the Laundry?'

'Another officer is already under orders. He will arrive this evening—may even have got here by now. I shall want to see him. There's a slight flap on, as a matter of fact.'

'What kind?'

'The Mobile Laundry have been ordered to stand in readiness to move at forty-eight hours' notice. This needs immediate attention with a new officer taking over only tonight. I was expecting the order in a week or two's time, not quite so soon as it has come. As usual, things will have to be done in a hurry.'

'Bithel was going anyway?'

'Of course—but only to the ITC. Now he will leave the army.'

'Is the Div moving?'

'The Laundry's orders have nothing to do with this formation, as such. There's been a call for Mobile Laundries. Between ourselves, I have reason to suppose this one is for the Far East, but naturally the destination is secret—and you are certainly not to mention that I hold that opinion.'

'You've known for some time they were going to move?'

'It came through to me when you were on leave.'

'You knew when you transferred Stringham?'

'That was precisely why I posted him to the Laundry.'

'So he'll go to the Far East?'

'If that's where the Laundry's bound.'

This was certainly arbitrary treatment of an old acquaintance.

'Will he want to go?'

'I have no idea.'

Widmerpool looked at me blankly.

'I suppose he could get out of it on grounds of age.'

'Why should he want to get out of it?'

'Well, he doesn't look as if his health is too good. As you said the other day, he's put away a good deal of drink in his time.'

'But it was you who suggested shifting him from his job as Mess Waiter,' said Widmerpool, not without impatience. 'That's one of the reasons I acted in the matter. I thought it over and decided, on balance, that you were right in feeling Stringham should not be there—in fact should not be at these Headquarters at all. Now you seem dissatisfied at what has happened. Why should it be your job—still less mine—to keep Stringham wrapped in cotton-wool? In any case, you surely don't envisage him remaining here after he and two of Div HQ's officers, one of them its DAAG, have been collectively concerned in putting another officer to bed because he has been found drunk in the street. You assured me Stringham would not be an embarrassment to us. That is exactly what has taken place.'

'But Stringham is quite used to the idea of drunks being put to bed. As he said last night, the pair of us once had to put him to bed ourselves. It couldn't conceivably affect Stringham's behaviour that he helped with Bithel—especially as Bithel's gone.'

'That has nothing to do with it.'

'What has then?'

'Nicholas, have you never heard of the word discipline?'

'But nobody knows except us—or was Biggs or somebody about when you got Bithel to G Mess?'

'No one—as it fortunately turned out. But that makes no difference whatever. Stringham could certainly not remain here after an incident of that kind. I applaud my own forethought in making the arrangement about him I did. So far as these Headquarters are concerned, the further afield he is sent the better. Let me add that all this is entirely a matter of principle. Stringham's presence would no longer affect me personally.'

'Why not?'

'Because I am leaving this formation.'

That piece of information brought a new, disturbing element into the conversation. I was annoyed, even disgusted, by Widmerpool's attitude towards Stringham, this utter disregard for what might happen to him, posted away to God knows where. However, worse now threatened. Self-interest, equally unattractive in outer guise and inner essence, is, all the same, a necessity for individual survival. It should perhaps not be too much despised, if only for that reason. Despised or not, its activities are rarely far from the surface. Now, at Widmerpool's words about leaving, I was unwelcomely conscious of self-interested anxieties throbbing hurriedly into operation. What was Widmerpool's present intention towards myself, if he were to go elsewhere? Would my fate be as little of interest to him as Stringham's? That was my instant thought.

'You've got promotion?'

'In the sense of immediate accession of rank—no. With the connotation that my employment will now be estab-lished in a more lofty—an incalculably more lofty—sphere than a Divisional Headquarters—yes.'

'The War Office?'

Widmerpool raised his hand slightly, at the same time allowing a brief smile to lighten his face in indication of the superiority, stratospheric in degree, towards which he was about to soar beyond the range of any institution so traditionally prosaic, not to say sordid in function, as the War Office. He folded his arms.

'No,' he said, 'not the War Office, I am thankful to say.'

'Where, then?'

'The Cabinet Offices.'

'I'm rather vague about them.'

'An admission that does not surprise me.'

'It's the top thing of all?'

'You might describe it that way.'

'How else?'

'The Cabinet Offices comprise, in one aspect, the area of action where the Ministry of Defence—the Chiefs of Staff, if you prefer—are in immediate contact with each other and with the Government of this country—with the Prime Minister himself.'

'I see.'

'So you will appreciate the fact that my removal of Stringham from these Headquarters will not affect me in the smallest way.'

'You go at once?'

'I have only heard unofficially at present. I imagine it will be the matter of a week, perhaps less.'

'Have you any idea what will happen to me when you're gone?'

'None.'

There was something impressive in his total lack of interest in the fate of all persons except himself. Perhaps it was not the lack of interest in itself—common enough to many people—but the fact that he was at no pains to conceal this within some more or less hypocritical integument.

'I shall be left high and dry?'

'I certainly doubt if my successor will be allocated an assistant. My own particular methods, more energetic than most, led to an abnormal amount of work for a mere DAAG. Even so, there has been recent pressure from above to encourage me to dispense with your services.'

'You haven't anything in mind for me?'

'Nothing.'

'You said you might try and fix something.'

'I have no recollection of doing so—and, anyway, what could I fix?'

'So it will be the Infantry Training Centre?'

'I should imagine.'

'Not much of a prospect.'

'The army more often than not offers uninviting prospects,' said Widmerpool. 'Look at the months I have been stuck here, wasting my time, and, if I may say so, my abilities. We are not soldiers just to enjoy ourselves. We are waging a war. You seem aggrieved. Let me point out there is nothing startlingly brilliant in your own work—your industry and capabilities—to make me press for a good appointment for you. In addition to what can only be regarded as mediocre qualities as a staff officer, it was you, and no other, who saw fit to involve me in the whole Bithel–Stringham hash. That might well have turned out very awkwardly for me. No, Nicholas, if you examine your conscience, you will find you have very little to grumble at.'

He sighed, whether at my own ingratitude or human frailty in general, I was uncertain. Cocksidge appeared in the doorway.

'A & Q wants to see you, sir,' he said. 'Right away. Very urgent. He's got the DAPM with him.'

'Right.'

'I hear you may be leaving us, sir,' said Cocksidge.

He spoke more with unction than servility.

'It's got round, has it?' said Widmerpool approvingly.

I had the impression he had put the rumour round himself. He went off down the passage. Cocksidge turned towards me, at the same time sharply adjusting his manner from that of lower-middle-grade obsequiousness to a major and staff officer, to one more in keeping for employment towards a second-lieutenant not even a member of the staff.

'The night you were last Duty Officer, Jenkins, the Field Park Company received their routine telephone contact five minutes later than the time noted on your report.'

'It went out in the normal manner with the others.'

'What happened then?'

'I suppose the Sapper Duty Officer didn't note it down immediately or else his watch was wrong.'

'I shall have to look into this,' said Cocksidge.

He spoke threateningly, as if expecting further explanation. I remembered now I had indeed effected the Field Park contact a few minutes later than the others for some trivial reason. However, I stuck to my guns. The matter was not of the smallest practical importance. If Cocksidge wanted to make trouble, he would have to undertake researches at some considerable labour to himself. That was unlikely with such meagre advantages in view. He left the room, slamming the door behind him. The telephone bell rang.

'Major Farebrother, from Command, downstairs, sir. Wants to see the DAAG.'

'Send him up.'

This was the first time Sunny Farebrother had ever paid a visit to Divisional Headquarters. Recently, he and Widmerpool had been less in conflict, less even in direct contact. Either old enmities had died down, or, I supposed, other more important matters had been occupying both of them. The news about himself Widmerpool had just released, in his own case confirmed that view. Farebrother was likely to have been similarly engaged, unless he had greatly changed. At that moment he came through the door, stopping short for a second, while he saluted with parade ground formality. Military psychology could to some extent be gauged by this business of saluting when entering a room. Officers of field rank would sometimes omit the convention, if, on entering, they immediately sighted only a subaltern there. These officers, one noticed, were often wanting when more serious demands were made on their capacity. However, few, even of those who knew how to behave, brought out the movement with such a click and snap as Farebrother had done. When he had relaxed, I explained Widmerpool had been summoned by Colonel

Pedlar and might be away from the office for some little time.

'I'm in no particular hurry,' said Farebrother. 'I had another appointment in the neighbourhood and thought I would look in on Kenneth. I'll wait, if I may.'

He accepted a chair. His manner was kindly but cold. He did not recognise me. There was little reason why he should after nearly twenty years, when we had travelled together to London after staying with the Templers. I remembered the taxi piled high with miscellaneous luggage and sporting equipment, as our ways had parted at the station. There had been a gun-case, a cricket bat and a fishing rod; possibly two squash racquets.

'You must come and lunch with me one of these days,' he had said, giving one of his very open smiles.

He was surprisingly unchanged from that moment. A suggestion of grey threaded, here and there, neat light-coloured hair. This faint powdering of silver increased the air of distinction, even of moral superiority, which his out-ward appearance always conveyed. The response he offered —that he was a person of self-denying, upright life—had nearly been allowed to become tinged with a touch of self-righteousness. Any such outgrowth was kept within bounds by the soldierly spruceness of his bearing. I judged him now to be in his early fifties. Middle-age caused him to look more than ever like one's conception of Colonel New-come, though a more sophisticated, enterprising prototype of Thackeray's old warrior. Sunny Farebrother could never entirely conceal his own shrewdness, however much he tried. He was a Colonel Newcome who, instead of collapsing into bankruptcy, had become, on retirement from the army, a brisk business executive; offered a seat on the East India Company's Board, rather than mooning round the precincts of the Charterhouse. At the same time, Farebrother would certainly know the right phrase to express appreciation of any such historic buildings or sentimental memories with which he might himself have been associated. One could be sure of that. He was not a player to overlook a useful card. Above all, he bestowed around him a sense of smoothness, ineffable, unstemmable smoothness, like oil flowing ever so gently from the spout of a vessel perfectly regulated by its pourer, soft lubricating fluid, gradually, but irresistibly, spreading; and spreading, let it be said, over an unexpectedly wide, even a vast area.

'What's your name?'

'Jenkins, sir.'

'Ah, we've spoken sometimes together on the telephone.'

Uniform—that of a London Territorial unit of Yeomanry cavalry—hardly changed Farebrother at all, unless to make him seem more appropriately clad. Cap, tunic, trousers, all battered and threadbare as his former civilian suits, had obviously served him well in the previous war. Frayed and shiny with age, they were far from making him look down-at-heel in any inadmissible way, their antiquity according a patina of impoverished nobility—nobility of the spirit rather than class—a gallant disregard for material things. His Sam Browne belt was limp with immemorial polishing. I recalled Peter Templer remarking that Farebrother's DSO had been 'rather a good one'; of the OBE next door to it, Farebrother himself had commented: 'told them I should have to wear it on my backside, as the only medal I've ever won sitting in a chair.' Whether or not he had in fact said any such thing, except in retrospect, he was well able to look after himself and his business in that unwarlike position, however assured he might also be in combat. It was not surprising Widmerpool hated him.

Leaning forward a little, puckering his face, as if even at this moment he found a sedentary attitude unsympathetic, he gazed at me suddenly as if he were dreadfully sorry about something.

'I've got some rather bad news for Kenneth, I'm afraid,' he said, 'but I expect I'd better keep it till he returns. I'd better tell him personally. He might be hurt otherwise.'

He spoke in a tone almost of misery. I thought the point had arrived when it should be announced that we had met before. Farebrother listened, with raised eyebrows and a beaming smile, while I briefly outlined the circumstances.

'That must have been seventeen or eighteen years ago.'

'Just after I'd left school.'

'Peter Templer,' he said. 'That's a curious coincidence.'

'You've heard about him lately?'

'I have, as a matter of fact. Of course I often used to run across him in the City before the war.'

'He's attached to some ministry now in an advisory capacity, isn't he?'

'Economic Warfare,' said Farebrother.

He fixed his very honest blue eyes on me. There was something a bit odd about the look.

'He told me he wasn't very happy where he was,' he said, 'and hearing I was making a change myself, thought I might be able to help.'

I did not see quite how Farebrother could help, but assumed that might be through civilian contacts, rather than from his own military status. Farebrother seemed to decide that he wanted to change the subject from Templer's immediate career, giving almost the impression that he felt he might himself have been indiscreet. He spoke quickly again.

'The old man died years ago, of course,' he said. 'He was an old devil, if ever there was one. Devil incarnate.'

I was a little surprised to hear Farebrother describe Peter Templer's father in such uncomplimentary terms, because, when we had met before, he had emphasised what a 'fine old man' he had thought Mr Templer; been positively sentimental about his good qualities, not to mention having contributed a laudatory footnote of personal memoir to the official obituary in *The Times*. I was more interested to talk of Peter than his father, but Farebrother would allow no further details.

'Said more than I should already. You surprised it out of me by mentioning the name so unexpectedly.'

'So you're leaving Command yourself, sir?'

'As I've begun being indiscreet, I'll continue on that line. I'm going to one of the cloak-and-dagger shows.'

From time to time one heard whispers of these mysterious sideshows radiating from out of the more normal activities of the Services. In a remote backwater like the Divisional Headquarters where I found myself, they were named with bated breath. Farebrother's apparent indifference to the prospect of becoming part of something so esoteric seemed immensely detached and nonchalant. Nevertheless, the manner in which he made this statement, in itself not in the least indiscreet, was at the same time perhaps a shade self-satisfied.

'Getting a step too,' he said. 'About time at my age.'

It was all at once clear as day that one of his reasons for coming round to Div HQ was to inform Widmerpool of this promotion to lieutenant-colonel. The discovery that we had known each other in the past had removed all coolness from Farebrother's manner. Now, he seemed, for some reason, even anxious to acquire me as an ally.

'How do you get on with our friend Kenneth?' he asked. 'A bit difficult at times? Don't you find that?'

I made no effort to deny the imputation. Widmerpool was grading low in my estimation at that moment. I saw no reason to conceal hard feelings about him. Farebrother was pleased at getting this affirmative reaction.

'I've no objection to a fellow liking to do things his own way,' he said, 'but I don't want a scrimmage about every new Army Council Instruction as soon as it appears. Don't you agree? In that sort of respect Kenneth doesn't know where to stop. Not only that, I found he's behaved rather badly behind my back with your Corps' MGA.'

It was news that Widmerpool's activities behind the scenes had taken him as far up in the hierarchy as so relatively august a personage as the Major-General in charge of Administration at Corps HQ.

'I mention that in confidence, of course,' said Farebrother, 'and for your own guidance. Kenneth can be a little thoughtless at times about his own subordinates. I daresay you've found that. Not that I would say a word against Kenneth as a man or a staff officer. In many ways he's wasted in this particular job.'

'He's leaving it.'

'He is?'

In spite of a conviction that Widmerpool's gifts were not being given sufficient scope, Farebrother did not sound altogether pleased to hear this matter was going to be put right. He asked the question with more open curiosity than he had showed until then.

'I don't think it's a secret.'

'Even if it is, it will go no further with me. What's ahead of him?'

'The Cabinet Offices, he told me, though I believe it's not official yet.'

Farebrother whistled, one of those crude expressions of feeling he would allow himself from time to time, which seemed hardly to accord with the dignity of the rest of his demeanour. I remembered him making a similar popping sound with his lips, at the same time snapping his fingers, when some beautiful woman's name had come into the conversation staying at the Templers'.

'The Cabinet Offices, by God,' he said. 'Has he been promoted?'

'I gather he goes there in his present rank, but thinks there's a good chance of going up pretty soon.'

'I see.'

Farebrother showed a little relief at Widmerpool's promotion being delayed, if only briefly. He had plainly been disturbed by what he had heard.

'*The Cabinet Offices,*' he repeated with emphasis. 'Well, that's very exalted. I only hope what I've come to tell him won't make any difference. However, as I said before, better not refer to that until I've seen him.'

He shook his head. Widmerpool came back to the room at that moment. He was fidgeting with the collar of his battle-dress, always a sign he was put out. It looked as if the interview with A & Q had not gone too well. Seeing Farebrother sitting there was not welcome to him either.

'Oh, hullo, Sunny,' he said, without much warmth.

'I came along to bid you farewell, Kenneth, and now I hear from Nicholas you're on the move like myself.'

Widmerpool showed a touch of surprise at Farebrother using my first name, then remembered we had formerly known each other.

'I forgot you'd both met,' he said. 'Yes, I'm going. Did Nicholas tell you where?'

'Scarcely revealed anything,' said Farebrother.

Not for the first time, I noted his caution, and was grateful for it, though Widmerpool seemed to want his destination known.

'The Cabinet Offices.'

Widmerpool could not conceal his own satisfaction.

'I say, old boy.'

The comparative enthusiasm Farebrother managed to infuse into this comment was something of a masterpiece in the exercise of dissimulation.

'It will mean work, morning, noon and night,' said Widmerpool. 'But there'll undoubtedly be interesting contacts.'

'There will, old boy, I bet there will—and promotion.'

'Possibly.'

'Quite soon.'

'Oh, you never know in the bloody army,' said Widmerpool, thought of his new job inducing a better humour, marked as usual by the assumption of his hearty military manner, 'but what's happening to you, Sunny, if you say you're going too?'

'One of these secret shows.'

'Baker Street?'

'I shouldn't be surprised.'

'Promotion too?'

Farebrother nodded modestly.

'That's the only reason I'm taking it. Need the pay. Much rather do something straightforward, if I had the choice.'

Widmerpool could not have been pleased to hear that Farebrother was about to become a lieutenant-colonel, while he himself, however briefly, remained a major. Indeed, it probably irritated him that Farebrother should be promoted at all. At the same time, a display of self-control rare with him, he contrived to show no concern, his manner being even reasonably congratulatory. This was no doubt partly on account of the satisfactory nature of his own promised change of employment, but, as he revealed on a later occasion, also because of the low esteem in which he held the organisation which Farebrother was about to join.

'A lot of scallywags, in my opinion,' he said later.

Farebrother was certainly acute enough to survey their respective future situations from much the same point of view, that is to say appreciating the fact that, although he might himself be now ahead, Widmerpool's potentialities for satisfying ambition must be agreed to enjoy a wider scope. Indeed, in a word or two, he openly expressed some such conclusion. Farebrother could afford this generosity, because, as it turned out, he had another trick up his sleeve. He brought this trump card out only after they had talked for a minute or two about their new jobs. Farebrother opened his attack by abruptly swinging the subject away from their own personal affairs.

'You've been notified Ivo Deanery's going to get the Recce Unit?' he asked suddenly.

Widmerpool was taken aback by this question. He began to look angry again.

'Never heard of him,' he said.

The answer sounded as if it were intended chiefly to gain time.

'Recently adjutant to my Yeomen,' said Farebrother. 'As lively a customer as you would meet in a day's march. Got an MC in Palestine just before the war.'

Widmerpool was silent. He did not show any interest at

all in Ivo Deanery's juvenile feats of daring, whatever they might have been. I supposed he did not want to admit to Farebrother that he himself had been running a candidate for the Recce Unit's Commanding Officer; and that candidate, from what had been said, must have been unsuccessful.

'Knew you were interested in the Recce Regiment command,' said Farebrother, speaking very casually.

'Naturally.'

'I mean specially interested.'

'There was nothing special about it,' said Widmerpool.

'Oh, I understood there was,' said Farebrother, assuming at once a puzzled expression, as if greatly worried at Widmerpool's denial of special interest. 'In fact that was the chief reason I came round to see you.'

'Look here,' said Widmerpool, 'I don't know what you're getting at, Sunny. How could you be DAAG of a formation and not take a keen interest in who's appointed to command its units?'

He was gradually losing his temper.

'The MGA thinks you were a bit too interested,' said Farebrother, speaking now with exaggerated sadness. 'Old boy, there's going to be the hell of a row. You've put your foot in it.'

'What do you mean?'

Widmerpool was thoroughly disturbed now, frightened enough to control his anger. Farebrother looked interrogatively at me, then his eyes travelled back to Widmerpool. He raised his eyebrows. Widmerpool shook his head vigorously.

'Say anything you like in front of him,' he said. 'He knows I had a name in mind for the Recce Unit command. Nothing wrong with that. Naturally I regret my chap hasn't got it. That's all there is to it. What's the MGA beefing about?'

Farebrother too shook his head, but slowly and more lugubriously than ever.

'I understand from the MGA that you were in touch with him personally not long ago about certain matters with which I myself was concerned.'

Widmerpool went very red.

'I think I know what you mean,' he said, 'but they were just as much my concern as yours.'

'Wouldn't it have been better form, old boy, to have mentioned to me you were going to see him?'

'I saw no cause to do so.'

Widmerpool was not at all at ease.

'Anyway,' said Farebrother mildly, 'the MGA, rightly or wrongly, feels you misled him about various scraps of unofficial information you tendered, especially as he had no idea at the time that you were pressing in other quarters for a certain officer to be appointed to a command then still vacant.'

'How did he find that out?'

'I told him,' said Farebrother, simply.

'But look here . . .' said Widmerpool.

He was too furious to finish the sentence.

'The long and the short of it was the MGA said he was going to get in touch with your General about the whole matter.'

'But I behaved in no way incorrectly,' said Widmerpool. 'There is not the smallest reason to suggest . . .'

'Believe me, Kenneth, I'm absolutely confident you did nothing to which official exception could possibly be taken,' said Farebrother. 'On my heart. That's why I thought it best to put my own cards on the table. The MGA is sometimes hasty. As you know well, amateur soldiers like you and me tend to go about our business in rather a different way from the routine a Regular gets accustomed to. We like to get things done expeditiously. I just thought it was a pity myself you went and told the MGA all those things about me. That was why I decided he ought to know more about you and your own activities. I'm sure everything will be all right in the end, but I believed it right to warn you—as I was coming to say goodbye anyway—simply that my General might be getting in touch with your General about all this.'

Farebrother's quiet, reassuring tone did not at all soothe Widmerpool, who now looked more disturbed than ever. Farebrother rose to his feet. He squared his shoulders and smiled kindly, pleased, as well he might be, with the devastation his few minutes' conversation had brought about in the promotion of Widmerpool's plans. In his own way, as I learnt later, Farebrother was an efficient operator when he wanted something done; very efficient indeed. Widmerpool had made a mistake in trying to double-cross him in whatever matter the visit to the MGA had concerned. He should have guessed that Farebrother, sooner or later, would find out. Perhaps he had disregarded that possibility, ruling out the risk of Farebrother turning to a formidable weapon at hand. However, with characteristic realism, Widmerpool grasped that something must be done quickly, if trouble, by now probably inevitable, was to be reduced in magnitude. He was not going to waste time in recrimination.

'I'll come with you to the door, Sunny,' he said. 'I can explain all that business about going to the MGA. It wasn't really aimed at you at all, though now I see it must look like that.'

Farebrother turned towards me. He gave a nod.

'Goodbye, Nicholas.'

'Goodbye, sir.'

They left the room together. The situation facing Widmerpool might be disagreeable, almost certainly was going to be. One thing at least was certain: whomsoever he had been trying to jockey into the position of commanding the Recce Unit would have done the job as well, if not better, than anyone else likely to be appointed. Widmerpool's candidate—if only for Widmerpool's own purposes—would, from no aspect, turn out unsuitable. If his claims were pressed by Widmerpool, he would be a first-class officer, not a personal friend whose competence was no more than adequate. That had to be said in fairness to Widmerpool methods, though I had no cause to like them. So far as that went, Farebrother's man, Ivo Deanery, as it turned out, made a good job of the command too. He led the Divisional Recce Corps, with a great deal of dash, until within a few days of the German surrender; then was blown up when his jeep drove over a landmine. However, that is equally by the way. The immediate point was that Widmerpool, even if his machinations had not actually transgressed beyond what were to be regarded as the frontiers of discipline, could, at the same time, well have allowed himself liberties with the established scope permissible to an officer of his modest rank, which, if brought to light, would seriously affront higher authority. Probably his original contact with the Major-General at Corps had been on the subject of a petty contention with Farebrother; something better not arranged—certainly better not arranged behind Farebrother's back; at the same time trivial enough. Widmerpool had no scruples about conduct of that sort.

'No good being too gentlemanly,' he had once said.

The next stage might be guessed. Having gained access to the MGA on this pretext, opportunity had been found to link the subject in hand with matters relating to the Recce Unit. Possibly the MGA was even glad to be provided with one or other of those useful items of miscellaneous private information which Widmerpool was so pre-eminent in storing up his sleeve for use at just that sort of interview. Then, so it seemed, something had gone wrong. The MGA had allowed Farebrother to find out, or at least make a good guess, that Widmerpool had been brewing up trouble for him. Like so many individuals who believe in being 'ungentlemanly', Widmerpool did not allow sufficiently for the eventuality of other people practising the same doctrine. Indeed, he used to complain bitterly if they did. Farebrother was an example of a man equally unprejudiced by scruple. No doubt he had pointed out to the MGA that Widmerpool's suggested line included contrivances that, when examined in the light of day, revealed—perhaps only to an over-fastidious sense of how things should be done—shreds of what might be regarded as the impertinent intrigue of a junior officer. That, at least, seemed to have been just how the MGA had seen the matter. He had become angry. Now, as Farebrother said, there was going to be the hell of a row; this at a most awkward juncture in Widmerpool's career. He was evidently having a longish talk with Farebrother on the doorstep. Before he returned Greening looked in.

'DAAG about?'

'Just gone down the stairs to have a final word with his opposite number from Command. He'll be back in a second.'

'His Nibs wants Major Widmerpool at once.'

'Shall I tell him?'

'I'll wait. His Nibs is far from pleased. Absolutely cheesed off, in fact. I don't dare go back without my man —like the North-West Mounted Police.'

'What's happened?'

'No idea.'

It looked as if the trouble in question was about to begin. Greening and I had a game of noughts and crosses. Widmerpool returned. Greening delivered his summons. Widmerpool, who was looking worried already, gave a slight twitch, but made no comment. He and Greening went off together in the direction of the General's room. In the army, long tracts of time when nothing whatever seems to happen are punctuated by sudden unexpected periods of upheaval and change. That is traditional. We had been all at once sucked into one of those whirlpools. Colonel Hogbourne-Johnson was the next person to enter the room. This was a rare occurrence, of which the most likely implication was that some sudden uncontrollable rage was too great to allow him to remain inactive while Widmerpool was summoned by telephone to his own presence. He must have come charging up the passage to prevent it boiling over without release, thereby perhaps doing him some internal injury. That turned out to be a wrong guess. The Colonel was, on the contrary, in an unusually good humour.

'Where's the DAAG?'

'With the Divisional Commander, sir.'

Colonel Hogbourne-Johnson took the chair on which Farebrother had been sitting a moment before. To remain was as unexpected as arrival here. There could be no doubt he was specially pleased about something. It might well be he already knew Widmerpool was in hot water. He pulled at his short, bristly, dun-coloured moustache.

'Aren't you some sort of a literary bloke in civilian life?' he asked.

I agreed that was the case.

'The General said something of the kind the other day.'

Colonel Hogbourne-Johnson emitted that curious sound, a kind of hissing gulp issuing from the corner of his mouth, after this comment, apparently, on this occasion, to express the ease he himself felt in the presence of the arts.

'I once wrote rather a good parody myself,' he said.

'You did, sir?'

'On Omar Khayyám.'

I indicated respectful interest.

'Quite amusing, it was,' said Colonel Hogbourne-Johnson, without apology.

I was about to entreat him to recite, if not all, at least a few quatrains of what promised to be an essay in pastiche well worth hearing, when Widmerpool's return prevented further exploration of the Colonel's Muse.

'Ah, Kenneth,' said Colonel Hogbourne-Johnson, assuming his most unctuous manner, 'I was hoping you would spare me a moment of your valuable time.'

Widmerpool looked even less pleased to see Hogbourne-Johnson than at Farebrother's visit. He was by now showing a good deal of wear and tear from the blows raining down on him.

'Yes, sir?' he answered tonelessly.

'Mr Diplock . . .' said Colonel Hogbourne-Johnson. 'No, you need not go, Nicholas.'

He sat on the chair banging his knees with his clenched fists, taking his time about what he wanted to say. It looked as if he desired a witness to be present at what was to be his humiliation of Widmerpool over the Diplock affair.

Use of my own christian name indicated an exceptionally good humour.

'Yes, sir?' repeated Widmerpool.

'I'm afraid you're going to be proved to have made a big mistake, my son,' said Colonel Hogbourne-Johnson.

He snapped the words out like an order on the parade ground. Widmerpool did not speak.

'Barking up the wrong tree,' said Colonel Hogbourne-Johnson.

Widmerpool pursed his lips and raised his eyebrows. Even in the despondent state to which he had been reduced, he was still capable of anger.

'You brought a series of accusations against an old and tried soldier,' said Colonel Hogbourne-Johnson, 'by doing so causing a great deal of unpleasantness, administrative dislocation and unnecessary work.'

Widmerpool began to speak, but the Colonel cut him short.

'I had a long talk with Diplock yesterday,' he said, 'and I am now satisfied he can clear himself completely. With that end in view, I sanctioned a day's leave for him to collect certain evidences. Now, I understand you may be leaving us?'

'I . . .'

Widmerpool hesitated. Then he pulled himself together.

'Yes, sir,' he said. 'I'm certainly leaving the Division.'

'Before you go,' said Colonel Hogbourne-Johnson, 'I consider it will be necessary for you to make an apology.'

'I don't yet know, sir,' said Widmerpool, 'the new facts which have come to light that should so much alter what appeared to be incontrovertible charges. I have been with A & Q earlier this afternoon, who told me you had made the arrangement you mention. He had informed the

DAPM, thinking Diplock should be kept under some general supervision.'

Even though he said that in a fairly aggressive tone, Widmerpool's manner still gave the impression that his mind was on other things. No doubt—his own fate in the balance—he found difficulty in concentrating on the Diplock case. It looked as if Colonel Hogbourne-Johnson, like a cat with a mouse, wanted to play with Widmerpool for a while before releasing information, because, instead of communicating anything he might know that had fresh bearing on Diplock and his goings-on, he changed the subject.

'Then there's another matter,' he said. 'Certain moves made with regard to the Reconnaissance Battalion.'

'The General has just been speaking on that subject too,' said Widmerpool.

Hogbourne-Johnson was plainly surprised at this admission. His expression showed he had no knowledge of the disturbance proceeding, at a higher level than his own, on the subject of Widmerpool's Recce Unit intrigues.

'To you?'

'Yes,' said Widmerpool bluntly. 'The General told me a Major—now, of course, Lieutenant-Colonel—Deanery has been appointed to that command.'

If he had hoped to score off Widmerpool in the Recce Unit sphere, it seemed Hogbourne-Johnson had over-reached himself. He reddened. No doubt he knew Widmerpool had been fishing in troubled waters, but was not up to date as to the outcome. If Widmerpool's candidate had been turned down, so too, it now appeared, had his own. This fact was most unacceptable to the Colonel. His manner changed from a peculiarly assertive, sneering self-assurance, to mere everyday bad temper.

'Ivo Deanery?'

'A cavalryman.'

'That's the one.'

'He's got the command.'

'I see.'

For the moment, Colonel Hogbourne-Johnson had nothing to say. He was absolutely furious, but could not very well admit he had just heard news that showed his own secret plans, whatever they were, had miscarried. That Widmerpool, whom he had come to harass, should be the vehicle of this particular item of information must have been additionally galling. However, something much worse from Hogbourne-Johnson's point of view, also much more dramatic, happened a second later. The door opened and Keef, the DAPM, came into the room. He was excited about something. Clearly looking for Widmerpool, not at all expecting to find Colonel Hogbourne-Johnson there, Keef appeared taken aback. A gnarled, foxy little man—like most DAPMs, not a particularly agreeable figure—he was generally accepted to handle soundly his section of Military Police, always difficult personnel of whom to be in charge. Now, he hesitated for a moment, trying to decide, so it seemed, whether, there and then, to make some disclosure he had on his mind, or preferably concoct an excuse, and retire until such time as he could find Widmerpool alone. Keef must have come to the conclusion that immediate announcement of unwelcome tidings would be best, because, straightening himself almost to the position of attention, he addressed Colonel Hogbourne-Johnson, as if it were Colonel Hogbourne-Johnson himself he had been looking for all the time. The reason for his momentary reluctance was revealed only too soon.

'Excuse me, sir.'

'Yes?'

'A serious matter has come through on the telephone, sir.'

'Well, what is it?'

'Diplock's deserted, sir.'

This message was so unexpected that Colonel Hogbourne-Johnson, already sufficiently provoked by the appointment of Ivo Deanery to the command of the Recce Unit, could find no words at first to register the fact that he fully comprehended what Keef had to report. The awfulness of the silence that followed must have told on Keef's nerves. Still standing almost to attention, it was he who spoke first.

'Just come through, sir,' he repeated. 'A & Q issued an order to keep an eye on him, but it was too late. The man's known to have made his way across the Border. He's in neutral territory by this time.'

To have trusted Diplock, to have stood by him when accused of peculation, was, so far as I knew from my own experience of Colonel Hogbourne-Johnson, the only occasion when he had ever shown a generous impulse. Of course that was speaking from scarcely any knowledge of him at all. In private life he may have displayed qualities concealed during this brief observation of his professional behaviour. Even if that were not so, and he were as unengaging to his friends and family as to his comrades in arms, even if, with regard to Diplock, his conduct had been dictated by egoism, prejudice, pig-headedness, the fact remained that he had believed in Diplock, had trusted him. He had, for example, called Widmerpool to order for describing the chief clerk as an old woman, simply because he respected the fact that Diplock, years before, had been awarded the Military Medal. Now he had been thoroughly let down. The climax had not been altogether deserved. Widmerpool had been wrong too. Diplock might be an old woman when he fiddled about with Army Forms; not when it came to evading his deserts. Still, that was another matter. It was Colonel Hogbourne-Johnson who had been betrayed. Possibly he felt that himself. He rose to his feet, in doing so managing to sweep to the floor some of the papers from the pile of documents on Widmerpool's table. Giving a jerk of his head to indicate Keef was to follow him, he left the room. Their steps could be heard thudding down uncarpeted passages. Widmerpool shut the door after them. Then he stooped and laboriously recovered several Summaries of Evidence from the floor. Anxiety about his own future was evidently too grave to allow any satisfaction at Hogbourne-Johnson's discomfiture. In fact, I had not seen Widmerpool so upset, so reduced to utter despair, since the day, long past, when he had admitted to paying for Gypsy Jones's 'operation'.

'There's been the devil of a row,' he said.

'What's happened?'

'The General's livid with rage.'

'About what Sunny Farebrother said?'

'That bloody MGA's given him a totally false picture of what I said.'

'What's the upshot?'

'General Liddament says he's going to make further enquiries. If he's satisfied I've behaved in a way of which he disapproves, he won't keep me on his staff. Of course I don't mind that, as I'm leaving anyway. What I'm worried about is he may take it into his head to ruin my chance of this much better job, when he gets official notification. He seemed to have forgotten that was in the air.'

'Does he know Hogbourne-Johnson was playing about with the same matter?'

'Of course not. Hogbourne-Johnson will be able to cover his tracks now.'

'And Diplock?'

'Oh, yes, Diplock,' said Widmerpool, cheering up a little. 'I'd forgotten about Diplock. Well, it was just as I said, though I'd never have guessed he'd go as far as to desert. Perhaps he wouldn't have deserted, if there hadn't been a frontier so conveniently near. This is all very worrying. Still, we must get on with some work. What have you got there?'

'The question of Mantle's name being entered for a commission has come up again.'

Widmerpool thought for a moment.

'All right,' he said, 'we'll by-pass Hogbourne-Johnson and send it in.'

He took the paper from me.

'And Stringham?'

'What about him?'

'If the Mobile Laundry are to be pushed off to the Far East, as you think——'

'Oh, bugger Stringham,' said Widmerpool, his mood suddenly changing. 'Why are you always fussing about Stringham? If he wants to get out of going overseas, he can probably do so at his age. That's his affair. Which reminds me, the officer replacing Bithel in charge of the Mobile Laundry should be reporting in an hour or so. I shall want you to take him round there and give him a preliminary briefing. I'll go into things myself in more detail later. He's called Cheesman.'

Nothing much else happened that afternoon. Widmerpool uttered one or two sighs to himself, but did not discuss his own predicament further. As he had said, there was nothing to be done. He could only wait and see how matters shaped. No one knew better than Widmerpool that, in the army, all things are possible. He might ride the storm. On the other hand, he could easily find himself packed off to a static appointment in West Africa, or another distant post unlikely to lead to the sort of promotion he had at present in mind. When Cheesman appeared later on, it was immediately clear that the Laundry, when proceeding overseas, was to have a very different commander from Bithel.

'I'm afraid I'm not quite so punctual as I intended, sir,' he said, 'but I'm anxious to get to work as soon as possible.'

Cheesman told me later he was thirty-nine. He looked quite ageless. Greying hair and wire spectacles suited his precise, rather argumentative manner of speech, in which he had not allowed the smallest trace of an army tone to alloy indefectibly civilian accents. Indeed, he spoke as if he had just arrived from a neighbouring firm to transact business with our own. He treated Widmerpool respectfully, as if a mere representative was meeting a managing director, but nothing in the least military supervened. Widmerpool might sometimes behave like this, but he also prided himself on the crispness of his own demeanour as a staff officer, and obviously did not greatly take to Cheesman. However, from whatever reports he had received about Cheesman's ability, he had evidently satisfied himself the job would be done in an efficient manner. After exchanging a few sentences regarding the taking-over of the Laundry, he told me to act as guide, after Cheesman's baggage had been delivered to G Mess. No doubt, in the prevailing circumstances, Widmerpool was glad to be left alone for a time to think things over.

'I'll have a word with you tomorrow, Cheesman,' he said, 'when you've a better idea of the Laundry's personnel and equipment, in relation to a move.'

'I shall be glad to have a look round, sir,' said Cheesman.

He and I set off together for the outer confines of the billeting area, where the Mobile Laundry had its being during spells at HQ. Cheesman told me he was an accountant in civilian life. He had done a good deal of work on laundry accounts at one time or another, accordingly, after getting a commission, had put in for a Mobile Laundry command.

'They seemed surprised I wanted to go to one,' he said. 'It struck me as only logical. The OC of my OCTU roared with laughter. He used to do that anyway when I spoke with him. He agreed I was too old for an infantry second-lieutenant and wanted me to go to the Army Pay Corps, or to train as a cipher officer, but in the end I got a Laundry. I hoped to command men. I was transferred to this one because my work seems to have been thought well of. I felt flattered.'

'You've got a first-rate sergeant in Ablett.'

'That's good news. My last one wasn't always too reliable.'

Sergeant Ablett was waiting for us. As Bithel had asserted in his drunken delirium, the Sergeant added to his qualities as an unusually efficient NCO those required for performing as leading comedian at the Divisional Concert, where he would sing forgotten songs, crack antediluvian jokes and dance unrestrainedly about the stage wearing only his underclothes. Ablett's was always the most popular turn. Now, however, this talent for vaudeville had been outwardly subdued, in its place assumed the sober, posi-

217

tively severe bearing of an old soldier, whose cleanshaven upper lip, faintest possible proliferation of side-whisker, perhaps consciously characterised a veteran of Wellington's campaigns. Contact was made between Cheesman and Ablett. It struck me that now would be a good opportunity to try and speak with Stringham.

'There's a man in your outfit I want a word with. May I do that while the Sergeant is showing you round?'

'By all means,' said Cheesman. 'Some personal matter?'

'He's a chap I know in civilian life.'

Cheesman was the sort of person to be trusted with that information. Anyway, the unit was moving. Sergeant Ablett summoned a corporal. I went off with him to find Stringham, leaving Cheesman to get his bearings.

'Last saw Stringy on his bed in the barrack room,' said the corporal, a genial bottle-nosed figure, who evidently did not take military formalities too seriously.

He went off through a door. I waited in a kind of yard, where the Mobile Laundry's outlandish vehicles were parked. In a minute or two the corporal appeared again. He was followed by Stringham, who looked as if the unexpected summons had made him uneasy. He was not wearing a cap. When he saw me, his face cleared. He came to attention.

'Thank you, Corporal.'

'You're welcome, sir.'

The bottle-nosed corporal disappeared.

'You gave me quite a turn, Nick,' Stringham said. 'I was lying on my bed musing about Tuffy and what a strange old girl she is. I was reading Browning, which always makes me think of her. Browning's her favourite poet. Did I tell you that? Of course I did, I'm getting hopelessly forgetful. He always makes me feel rather jumpy. That was why I got in a flap when Corporal Treadwell said I was wanted by an officer.'

'I've just brought your new bloke round who's taken Bithel's place.'

'Poor Bith. That was an extraordinary evening last night. What's happened to him?'

'Widmerpool's shot him out.'

'Dear me. Just as well, perhaps, for the army's sake, but I shall miss him. What's this one like?'

'He's called Cheesman. Should be easy to handle if you stay with him.'

'Why shouldn't I stay with him? I'm wedded to the Laundry by this time. I've really begun to know the meaning of *esprit de corps*, something lamentably lacking in me up to now.'

'I want to talk about all that.'

'*Esprit de corps?*'

'Can't we take a stroll for a couple of minutes while Cheesman deals with your Sergeant?'

'Ablett's a great favourite of mine too,' said Stringham. 'I'm trying to memorise some of his jokes for use at dinner parties after the war, if I'm ever asked to any again— indeed, if any are given *après la guerre*. Ablett's jokes have an absolutely authentic late nineteenth-century ring that fills one with self-confidence. Wait a moment, I'll get a cap.'

When he returned, wearing a side-cap, he carried in his hand a small tattered volume. We walked slowly up an endless empty street of mean redbrick houses. The weather, for once, was warm and sunny. Stringham held up the book.

'Before we part, Nick,' he said, 'I must read you something I found here. I can't make out just what all of it means, but some has obvious bearing on army life.'

'Charles, you've got to do some quick thinking. The Mobile Laundry is due to move.'

'So we heard.'

'There've been rumours?'

'One always knows these things first in the ranks. That's one of the advantages. Where's it to be?'

'Of course that's being kept secret, but Widmerpool thinks—for what it's worth—the destination is probably the Far East.'

'We heard that too.'

'Then you know as much as me.'

'We seem to. Of course, security may be so good, it will really turn out to be Iceland. That sort of thing is always happening.'

'The point is, you could probably—certainly—get out of being sent overseas on grounds of age and medical category.'

'I agree I'm older than the rocks amongst which I sit, and have died infinitely more times than the vampire. Even so, I'd quite like to see the gorgeous East—even the Icelandic geysers, if it comes to that.'

'You'll go through with it?'

'Not a doubt.'

'I just thought I ought to pass on what was being said—strictly against all the rules.'

'That shan't go any further. Depend upon it. I suppose Widmerpool saw this coming?'

'So I gather.'

'And all that altruism about F Mess was to get me on the move?'

'That's about it.'

'He couldn't have done me a better turn,' said String-ham. 'The old boy's a marvellous example of one of the aspects of this passage I want to read you. Like everything that's any good, it has about twenty different meanings.'

He stopped and began turning the pages of the book he had brought with him. We stood beside a pillar-box. When he found the place, he began to read aloud:

> 'I shut my eyes and turned them on my heart.
> As a man calls for wine before he fights,
> I asked one draught of earlier, happier sights
> Ere fitly I could hope to play my part.
> Think first, fight afterwards—the soldier's art;
> One taste of the old time sets all to rights.'

'Childe Roland to the Dark Tower came?'
'Childe Stringham—in this case.'
'I'm never sure what I feel about Browning.'
'He always gives the impression of writing about people who are wearing very expensive fancy dress. All the same, there's a lot in what he says. Not that I feel in the least nostalgic about earlier, happier sights. I can't offhand re-call many. The good bit is about thinking first and fighting after.'

'Let's hope the High Command have taken the words to heart.'
'Odd that Browning should know that was so important.'
'Perhaps he should have been a general.'
'It ought to be equally borne in mind by all ranks. There might be an Order of the Day on the subject. Can't Wid-merpool arrange that?'
'Widmerpool's leaving Div HQ too.'
'To become a colonel?'

'The Divisional Commander may bitch that up. He's tumbled on some of Widmerpool's intriguing and doesn't approve, but Widmerpool will go either way.'

'How very dramatic.'

'Isn't it.'

'Then what will happen to you?'

'God knows. The ITC, I imagine. Look, I shall have to go back to Cheesman soon, but I must tell you about the hell of a business on my leave the other day.'

I gave some account of the bombing of the Madrid and the Jeavons house.

'The Madrid, fancy that. I once took Peggy there in the early days of our marriage. The evening was a total frost. And then where I used to live in that top floor flat with Tuffy looking after me—where I learnt to be sober. Where Tuffy used to read Browning. Is it all in ashes?'

'Not in the least. The outside of the house looks just the same as usual.'

'Poor Lady Molly—she ought to have stayed doing that job at Dogdene.'

'Much too quiet for her.'

'Poor Ted, too. What on earth will he do with himself now? I used to enjoy occasionally sneaking off to the pub with Ted.'

'He's going on as before. Camping out in the house and carrying on as an air-raid warden.'

'I chiefly remember your sister-in-law, Priscilla, as making rather good going with some musician for whom my mother once gave an extraordinary party. Weren't you there, Nick? I associate that night with an odd little woman covered in frills like Little Bo-Peep. I made some sort of dive at her.'

'She was called Mrs Maclintick. She's now living with

the musician for whom your mother gave the party—Hugh Moreland.'

'Moreland, that was the name. She's living with him, is she? What lax morals people have these days. The war, I suppose. I do my best to set an example, but no one follows me in my monastic celibacy. That was a strange night. Tuffy arrived to drive me home. It comes back to me fairly clearly, in spite of a great deal too much to drink. That's a taste of old times, if ever there was one. Makes one ready to fight anybody.'

'Charles, I shall have to get back to Cheesman. You've absolutely decided to stick to the Mobile Laundry, come what may?'

'*Quis separabit?*—that's the Irish Guards, isn't it? The Mobile Laundry shares the motto.'

'Are you returning to the billet?'

'I think I'll go for a stroll. Don't feel like any more poetry reading at the moment. Poetry always rather disturbs me. I think I shall have to give it up—like drink. A short walk will do me good. I'm off duty till nine o'clock.'

'Goodbye, Charles—if we don't meet before the Laundry moves.'

'Goodbye, Nick.'

He smiled and nodded, then went off up the street. He gave the impression of having severed his moorings pretty completely with anything that could be called everyday life, army or otherwise. I returned to Cheesman and Sergeant Ablett. They seemed to have got on well together and were still vigorously discussing vehicle maintenance.

'Find that man all right, sir?' asked the Sergeant.

'Had a word with him. Know him in civilian life.'

'Thought you might, sir. He could have been of use in

the concert, but now it looks as if we're moving and there won't be any concert.'

'I expect you'll put on a show wherever you go. We shall miss your trouserless tap-dance next time, Sergeant.'

'That's always a popular item,' said Sergeant Ablett, without false modesty.

I took Cheesman back to G Mess. His mildness did not prevent him from being argumentative about every subject that arose.

'That's what you think,' he said, more than once, 'but there's another point of view entirely.'

This determination would be useful in running the Laundry, subject, like every small, more or less independent entity, to all sorts of pressures from outside.

'Wait a moment,' he said. 'Before I forget, I'd like to make a note of your name, and the Sergeant's, and the DAAG's.'

He loosened the two top buttons of his service-dress tunic to rummage for a notebook. This movement revealed that he wore underneath the tunic a khaki waistcoat cut like that of a civilian suit. I commented on the unexpectedness of this garment, worn with uniform and made of the same material.

'You're not the first person to mention that,' said Cheesman unsmilingly. 'I can't see why.'

'You just don't see waistcoats as a rule.'

'I've always worn one up to now. Why should I stop because I'm in the army?'

'No reason at all.'

'Even the tailor seemed surprised. He said: "We don't usually supply a vest with service-dress, sir." '

'It's a tailor's war, anyway.'

'What do you mean?'

'That's just a thing people say.'

'Why?'

'God knows.'

Cheesman looked puzzled, but pursued the matter no further.

'See you at Church Parade tomorrow.'

Sunday morning was always concerned with getting the Defence Platoon on parade, together with the Military Police and other miscellaneous troops who make up Divisional Headquarters. This parade was not without its worries, because the Redcaps, most of them ex-guardsmen, marched at a more leisurely pace than the Line troops, some of whom, Light Infantry or Fusiliers, were, on the other hand, unduly brisk. Colonel Hogbourne-Johnson, whose sympathies were naturally with the 'Light Bobs' was always grumbling about its lack of progressional uniformity. That day all went well. After these details had been dismissed, I went to the DAAG's office to see if anything had to be dealt with before Monday. As it happened, I had spoken with none of the other officers after church. Widmerpool was not in his room, nor had he been present at the service. It was not uncommon for him to spend Sunday morning working, so that he might already have finished what he wanted to do and gone back to the Mess. Almost as soon as I arrived there the telephone bell rang.

'DAAG's office—Jenkins.'

'It's A & Q. Is the DAAG there?

'No, sir.'

'Has he been in this morning?'

'Not since I came here from Church Parade, sir.'

Colonel Pedlar sounded in an agitated state, it was hard to tell whether pleased or angry.

'Was the DADMS in church?'

'Yes, sir.'

I had noticed Macfic a few pews in front of where I was sitting.

'I can't get any reply from his room. Tell the man on the switch-board to try and find Major Widmerpool and Major Macfie and send them to me—and come along yourself.'

'Yes, sir.'

Colonel Pedlar was walking up and down his room.

'Have you told them to find the DADMS?'

'Yes, sir.'

'There's not much we can do until he arrives. A very unfortunate thing's happened. A tragedy, in fact. Most unpleasant.'

'Yes, sir?'

'The fact is the SOPT's hanged himself in the cricket pavilion.'

'That hut on the sports field, sir?'

'That's it. The one they lost the key of.'

Colonel Pedlar continued to stride backwards and forwards across his office.

'There's nothing much to be done until the DAAG and the DADMS arrive,' he said.

'When was this discovered, sir?'

'Only a short time ago—by a civilian who had to fetch some benches from the place.'

Colonel Pedlar stopped for a moment. Talking seemed to have relieved his feelings. Then he began to move again.

'What do you think of the news?' he asked.

'Well, it's rather awful, sir. Biggs was in my Mess—'

'Oh, I don't mean Biggs,' he said. 'Haven't you seen a paper or heard the wireless this morning? Germany's invaded Russia.'

An immediate, overpowering, almost mystic sense of relief took shape within me. I felt suddenly sure everything was going to be all right. This was something quite apart from even the most cursory reflection upon strategic implications involved.

'I give the Russians three weeks,' said Colonel Pedlar. 'If you haven't heard that the German army's attacked Russia, you probably don't know General Liddament has been given command of a Corps.'

'I didn't, sir.'

'He left this morning to take over at once.'

I had never known Colonel Pedlar so talkative. He was no doubt trying to keep his mind off Biggs by imparting all this information, while he wandered about the room.

'And we're going to lose our DAAG.'

'I'd heard he might be leaving, sir.'

'Though the posting hasn't come through yet.'

'No, sir?'

Colonel Pedlar ceased pacing up and down. He sat in his chair, holding his hand to his head.

'There was something else I wanted to talk to you about,' he said. 'Now what was it?'

I waited. The Colonel began looking among the papers on his table. More than ever his face was reminiscent of a dog sniffing about for a lost scent. Suddenly he picked it up and took hold of a scrap of paper.

'Ah, yes,' he said. 'About your own disposal.'

'Yes, sir?'

'You were going to the ITC.'

'Yes, sir.'

'But I've just had this. It should go through the DAAG, of course, but as you're here, you may as well see it.'

He handed across a teleprint message. It quoted my

name, rank, number, instructing me to report to a room, number also quoted, in the War Office the following week.

'I don't know anything about this,' said Colonel Pedlar.

'Nor me, sir.'

'Anyway it solves the problem of what's going to happen to you.'

'Yes, sir.'

At that moment, Widmerpool and Macfie came into the room. Macfie looked as glum as ever, if possible, glummer, but Widmerpool's face showed he had received news of the General's promotion and departure. His manner to Colonel Pedlar indicated that too, when the Colonel began to outline the circumstances of the suicide.

'I don't think Jenkins needs to stay, does he?' Widmerpool asked brusquely.

'I hardly think he does,' said Pedlar. 'You may as well go now. Don't forget to take necessary action about that signal I passed you.'

I went back to F Mess. Soper was discussing with Keef what had happened. His heavy simian eyebrows contorted in agitation, he looked more than ever like a professional comedian.

'A fine kettle of fish,' he said. 'Never thought Biggy would have done that. In the cricket pav, of all places, and him so fond of the game. Worrying about that key did it. More than the wife business, in my opinion. Quite a change it will be, not having him grousing about the food every day.'

That same week the plane was shot down in which Barnby was undertaking a reconnaissance flight with the aim of reporting on enemy camouflage.

A LIST OF ANTHONY POWELL TITLES
AVAILABLE FROM MANDARIN

☐ Afternoon Men	£5.99
☐ Venusberg	£5.99
☐ From a View to a Death	£5.99
☐ Agents and Patients	£5.99
☐ What's Become of Waring?	£5.99
☐ O, How the Wheel Becomes it	£5.99
☐ The Fisher King	£5.99

A Dance to the Music of Time

☐ A Question of Upbringing	£5.99
☐ A Buyer's Market	£5.99
☐ The Acceptance World	£5.99
☐ At Lady Molly's	£5.99
☐ Cassanova's Chinese Restaurant	£5.99
☐ The Kindly Ones	£5.99
☐ The Valley of Bones	£5.99
☐ The Soldier's Art	£5.99
☐ The Military Philosophers	£5.99
☐ Books Do Furnish A Room	£5.99
☐ Temporary Kings	£5.99
☐ Hearing Secret Harmonies	£5.99
☐ A Dance to the Music of Time Vol 1, Spring	£9.99
☐ A Dance to the Music of Time Vol 2, Summer	£9.99
☐ A Dance to the Music of Time Vol 3, Autumn	£9.99
☐ A Dance to the Music of Time Vol 4, Winter	£9.99

ALL ARROW BOOKS ARE AVAILABLE THROUGH MAIL ORDER OR FROM YOUR LOCAL BOOKSHOP AND NEWSAGENT.

PLEASE SEND CHEQUE / EUROCHEQUE / POSTAL ORDER (STERLING ONLY) ACCESS, VISA, MASTERCARD, DINERS CARD, SWITCH OR AMEX.

EXPIRY DATE .... SIGNATURE ....

PLEASE ALLOW 75 PENCE PER BOOK FOR POST AND PACKING U.K.

OVERSEAS CUSTOMERS PLEASE ALLOW £1.00 PER COPY FOR POST AND PACKING.

ALL ORDERS TO:

ARROW BOOKS, BOOK BY POST, TBS LIMITED, THE BOOK SERVICE, COLCHESTER ROAD, FRATING GREEN, COLCHESTER, ESSEX CO7 TDW.

NAME ....

ADDRESS ....

....

Please allow 28 days for delivery. Please tick box if you do not wish to receive any additional information ☐

Prices and availability subject to change without notice.